F. SCOTT FITZGERALD
and his contemporaries

F. SCOTT FITZGERALD *and* *his contemporaries*

WILLIAM GOLDHURST

THE WORLD PUBLISHING COMPANY
Cleveland and New York

GRATEFUL ACKNOWLEDGMENT is made to the following for their permission
to reprint from the works indicated: Random House, Inc.: Introduction to
The Great Gatsby, by F. Scott Fitzgerald, copyright 1934 and renewed
1961 by Random House, Inc. Doubleday & Company, Inc.: *A Parody
Outline of History* by Donald Ogden Stewart, copyright 1921 by George
H. Doran Co. Harcourt, Brace & World, Inc.: *Collected Poems of T. S.
Eliot*, copyright 1936 by Harcourt, Brace & World, Inc.; and *Between
Friends: Letters of James Branch Cabell and Others*, © 1962 by Har-
court, Brace & World, Inc. New Directions, Publishers: *The Crack-Up*
by F. Scott Fitzgerald (ed. by Edmund Wilson), copyright 1945 by New
Directions. Ben Roth Agency, Inc.: "To the Comfort Station," © Punch,
London. Charles Scribner's Sons: Extracts from the following works by
F. Scott Fitzgerald: *Afternoon of an Author, The Beautiful and Damned,
Flappers and Philosophers, The Great Gatsby, The Last Tycoon, Six Tales
of the Jazz Age, The Short Stories of F. Scott Fitzgerald, Tender Is the
Night, This Side of Paradise, The Vegetable,* copyright 1920, 1922, 1925,
1933, 1934, 1941, 1951 Charles Scribner's Sons. Copyright 1948, 1950,
1951, 1953, 1957, © 1961, 1962 Frances Scott Fitzgerald Lanahan. Copyright 1948 Zelda Fitzgerald. From *Round Up* by Ring Lardner, copyright
1929 Charles Scribner's Sons, renewal copyright © 1957 by Mrs. Ellis A.
Lardner; from *Gullible's Travels* by Ring Lardner, copyright 1926 by
Charles Scribner's Sons, renewal copyright 1954 by Mrs. Ellis A. Lardner;
from *Big Town* by Ring Lardner, copyright 1925 by Charles Scribner's
Sons, renewal copyright 1953 by Mrs. Ellis A. Lardner. From *The Col-
lected Essays of John Peale Bishop,* edited by Edmund Wilson, copyright
1948 Charles Scribner's Sons. From *Of Making Many Books* by Roger
Burlingame, copyright 1946 Charles Scribner's Sons. From *Editor to
Author: The Letters of Maxwell E. Perkins,* edited by John Hall
Wheelock, copyright 1950 Charles Scribner's Sons. Excerpts from the
following works by Ernest Hemingway: *Green Hills of Africa, The Sun
Also Rises, To Have and Have Not, The Fifth Column and the First
Forty-Nine Stories* (now published as *The Short Stories of Ernest
Hemingway*); copyright 1926, Charles Scribner's Sons; renewal copy-
right 1954 Ernest Hemingway; copyright 1935 Charles Scribner's Sons,
renewal copyright © 1963 Mary Hemingway; copyright 1937 Ernest
Hemingway.

Published by The World Publishing Company
2231 West 110th Street, Cleveland 2, Ohio
Published simultaneously in Canada by
Nelson, Foster & Scott Ltd.
Library of Congress Catalog Card Number: 63-8978
First Edition

For Barney and Rex
And especially for Judy

CONTENTS

FOREWORD

"True criticism," remarks Alfred Kazin, "only begins with books, but can never be removed from their textures. It begins with workmanship, talent, craft, but is nothing if it does not go beyond them." My own interest in the novels and stories of F. Scott Fitzgerald was the true beginning of this study. Like so many university students of the past fifteen years, I was easily and willingly captivated by Fitzgerald's workmanship, talent, craft; and many of his unerring phrases became an unforgettable part of my education. But in the pages that follow I do indeed go beyond these qualities, for a relatively broad perspective is necessary if we are to understand Fitzgerald's achievement.

Fitzgerald, of course, has already been subjected to close scrutiny from a variety of approaches. His friends have left reminiscences which give us an intimate understanding of the man's personal habits and history. Fitzgerald himself wrote a series of remarkably candid autobiographical essays which add considerably to that understanding. Arthur Mizener's pioneering biography provided a full and richly detailed account of the novelist's life and career, while a recent

book by Andrew Turnbull has added a surprising amount
of new material to a subject already well documented. From
these works and others, persons interested can easily acquire
elaborate information on Fitzgerald's schooling, his early
success, his reckless ways with money, his fondness for cock-
tail parties, his struggle against alcoholism, his wife's mental
collapse, his love affairs, and his unfortunate decline during
the last few years of his life. At the same time critical commentary on Fitzgerald's fiction is fairly extensive and varied.
While the most persistent critical strain has been biographical, a number of essays and books have explored the novelist's works from a sociological, textual, or historical point of
view. Few of Fitzgerald's contemporaries, in fact, have been
accorded such sustained and detailed treatment. Confronted
with all this biography and criticism, students of Scott Fitzgerald might justifiably wonder if anything relevant remains to be said on the subject.

I believe, obviously, that a great deal does remain to be
said about this writer whose works have become increasingly popular and important during the last two decades. It
might be helpful to my readers if I make a few prefatory
remarks about my procedure and intentions. As my own
interest in Fitzgerald deepened, so did my awareness of the
interconnections between his life and his art. From the
beginning, however, I resisted the doctrine—so often mis-
used of late—that fiction is a form of disguised and embel-
lished autobiography; there has been more than enough
emphasis on the idea that Fitzgerald told his own life story,
and the life story of Zelda, over and over again in his novels
and tales. I think it important now to balance the account
by showing Fitzgerald in a different light; by showing that
although he did indeed distill his personal experience into
his works, he also derived a large proportion of his material
from other sources. Fitzgerald's life in fact was a continu-

ous, deliberate effort to refine his artistic competence and to increase his understanding of experience other than his own. Fitzgerald sought development. He wanted greater perfection of style and more complete knowledge of the materials available for fiction. For instruction in such matters Fitzgerald turned to the source which sooner or later compels the attention of all serious writers in varying degrees of absorption—he turned to the works of other writers. To say that he was particularly susceptible to influence, and especially to the influence of writers whom he knew personally, is to suggest the theme of the present study. Placed side by side with his contemporaries, Scott Fitzgerald emerges as a unique quantity in recent American literature, but he also takes shape as an inseparable part of a literary generation and its ideas.

To explore Fitzgerald's development in the light of these contentions, I have adopted a method which I hope will do at least partial justice to the complexity of the subject. The contemporary writers who influenced Fitzgerald most significantly were four: Edmund Wilson, H. L. Mencken, Ring Lardner, and Ernest Hemingway. To each of these writers and the part he played in Fitzgerald's life I have devoted a chapter. And since Fitzgerald's involvements with these men were both personal and professional, I have tried to examine them as fully as the available evidence allows. Each chapter takes up Fitzgerald's personal relations with the writer concerned, calls attention to the affinities in the works of the two authors, and attempts to show specific points of influence, which on occasion was reciprocal. My intention throughout is to show Scott Fitzgerald as an artist in the process of continual and dynamic development, and as an active member of an incredibly vital literary community. If I succeed at all perhaps I can effect some slight revision of a damaging and irrelevant attitude which has often exhibited Fitzgerald as a writer of "natural" or "intuitive" talent, a cocktail-party habitué whose creative achievements were more or less incidental episodes in a life devoted to champagne, adventure, and social recklessness. These elements comprise a part of the story, to be sure, but: emphasis, emphasis.

A few words about inclusions and omissions. All his life Fitzgerald formed deep attachments to men who were dedicated, as he was, to the literary craft; and for many of the editors, poets, novelists, and storytellers of his acquaintance he had profound respect. He listened to their counsel. He studied their works. He adopted as his own many of their perspectives and ideas. More specifically, Fitzgerald derived a number of important benefits from his literary companions. They gave him encouragement and advice; they helped, at the start of his career, to get him published; they reviewed his novels in the popular magazines of the day; they provided him with the inspiration for many of his fictional characters; they informed him on issues that he later incorporated into his novels and stories; they advised him on matters of technique. In a significant sense, Fitzgerald's friends helped establish the direction and tendency of his fiction from start to finish. Wilson, Mencken, Lardner, and Hemingway were the chief participants in the drama. But there were others who stirred Fitzgerald's imagination, notably John Peale Bishop and Maxwell Perkins, whom I have not included here for various reasons: the specific influence was inconsiderable, or it was difficult to define without undue speculation, or the lack of available data makes an extended treatment impracticable. I have concentrated, therefore, on those writers with whom Fitzgerald was on terms of close friendship, and who left an impression on his work that is both manifest and significant.

But Fitzgerald's literary companionships, his indebted-

ness to the ideas of his contemporaries, and his development during successive stages of his career—these are but
parts of a larger story. The literature of the 1920s, which
forms the substance of the materials here considered, is so
closely bound to its era that all efforts to separate the two,
even by the most obstinate of the "pure" critics, will forever
be incomplete, if not entirely futile. Fitzgerald and his
contemporaries produced works of art, to be sure, and not
documentaries; but their principal subjects remain rooted
in the actual events and attitudes of their time. Furthermore,
the spirit of mutual interest among writers of the period is
a part of history too; at no other point in our tradition has
there been such an atmosphere of intimacy, of shared exchange and stimulation. These are the qualities largely
responsible for the enduring literature these men produced.
It is no accident that more and more recent historians, biographers, and critics have turned to the twenties to rediscover
the abundance and excitement of those years; it is rather a
tribute to a kind of vitality conspicuously absent from the
literary scene today. So the true protagonist of this account
is not Scott Fitzgerald, who forms only a focal point of
reference, but the age itself. In my first chapter I have
attempted to crystallize its spirit by portraying some few of
the interconnections, both personal and literary, among
writers of the twenties and early thirties. But I hope the
reader's initial impression of the setting will linger into
succeeding chapters to inform the whole drama.

It is a pleasure to acknowledge my indebtedness to the
Southern Fellowships Fund for a generous grant that enabled me to undertake a great deal more research than
would otherwise have been possible. The Southern Fellowships Fund, however, is not responsible for the opinions
expressed here. I should also like to thank the Directors of

Princeton University Library for permission to examine the documents contained in The F. Scott Fitzgerald Papers, which forms an impressive section of their Department of Rare Books and Special Collections.

Several individuals courteously submitted to interviews on the subject of Scott Fitzgerald's life and works. Among these are Carlos Baker, Chairman of the Department of English at Princeton; Arnold Gingrich, editor of *Esquire* magazine; Budd Schulberg; and the late Harold Ober, for many years Fitzgerald's friend and literary agent.

In addition to those individuals and firms noted on the copyright page, I should also like to express my gratitude to the following publishers and authors for permission to quote copyrighted material: Harper & Row for *Only Yesterday*, by Frederick Lewis Allen; John Abbot Clark and Twayne Publishers, Inc., for "The Love Song of F. Scott Fitzgerald" in *American Literature in Parody*, Robert P. Falk, ed.; Charles Angoff for *H. L. Mencken: A Portrait from Memory*, by Charles Angoff, Thomas Yoseloff, Publisher; Carlos Baker for *Hemingway: The Writer as Artist*, Princeton University Press; Donald Elder for *Ring Lardner*, by Donald Elder, Doubleday & Company, Inc.; Harcourt, Brace, & World, Inc., for *On Native Grounds*, by Alfred Kazin; Philip Horton for *Hart Crane: The Life of an American Poet*, by Philip Horton, W. W. Norton & Company, Inc.; John Richard Kuehl for "Scott Fitzgerald's Reading," *Princeton University Library Chronicle*, XXII:2 (Winter, 1961), 58-89 and "Scott Fitzgerald's Critical Opinions," *Modern Fiction Studies*, VII:1 (Spring, 1961), 3-18; Alfred A. Knopf, Inc., for *Prejudices: First Series* and *Prejudices: Second Series*, by H. L. Mencken; The Viking Press for *Studies in Classic American Literature*, by D. H. Lawrence; Arthur Mizener and Houghton Mifflin Company for *The Far Side of Paradise* by Arthur Mizener; Editors of *Esquire* for "Old Scott:

The Mask, the Myth, and the Man," by Budd Schulberg, *Esquire* LV:1 (January 1961), 96-101; Edmund Wilson for *Classics and Commercials* and *The Shores of Light*, by Edmund Wilson, Farrar, Straus and Young, Inc.; Glenway Wescott for "The Moral of F. Scott Fitzgerald" in *F. Scott Fitzgerald: The Man and His Work*, Alfred Kazin, ed., The World Publishing Company; Mrs. James Branch Cabell for *Between Friends: Letters of James Branch Cabell and Others.*

In addition, I would like to thank the following for generous permission to quote unpublished letters to Fitzgerald: Thornton Wilder, Estate of Louis Bromfield, Jonathan Bishop (John Peale Bishop), Estate of Marjorie Kinnan Rawlings, Peggy Wood Weaver Walling (John V. A. Weaver), Laura West Perelman (Nathanael West), Mrs. Maxwell Perkins and Charles Scribner's Sons, Ring Lardner, Jr., Edmund Wilson, John Dos Passos. And Gilbert Seldes (letter to Tristan Tzara), Katherine Gauss Jackson and Carlos Baker (letters from Christian Gauss to Mr. Baker), Donald Ogden Stewart and Carlos Baker (letter from Mr. Stewart to Mr. Baker), and T. S. Eliot and Charles Scribner's Sons (statement from dust jacket of *Tender Is the Night*).

Finally, I should like to make special mention of my debt to Samuel Hurwitz, of the Department of History at Brooklyn College; to Maxwell Geismar; and to George W. Meyer and Richard Harter Fogle, both of the English Department Faculty at Tulane University. These gentlemen read my manuscript, entire or in part, and offered valuable suggestions for revision.

WILLIAM GOLDHURST

University of Puerto Rico
Rio Piedras, P.R.

F. SCOTT FITZGERALD
and his contemporaries

*I am certain that a number of us at least
have some kind of community of interest.
And with this communion will come
something better than a mere clique. It is
a consciousness of something more than
stylistic questions and "taste," it is a vision,
and a vision alone that not only America
needs but the whole world.*

—HART CRANE

CHAPTER I

Time, Place, and Spirit

> She sleeps—eternal Helen—in the moonlight
> of a thousand years; immortal symbol of
> immortal aeons, flower of the gods
> transplanted on a foreign shore, infinitely
> rare, infinitely erotic.
>
> —DONALD OGDEN STEWART

Donald Ogden Stewart's *A Parody Outline of History* provides a humorous but illuminating survey of some major episodes in the literary life of the nineteen-twenties. Published in 1921, Stewart's deft satire uncovers the ludicrous excesses that lay just beneath the surface of the books America was reading. "Main Street: Plymouth, Mass." reduces Sinclair Lewis's famous novel to absurdity, accurately noting Carol Kennicott's febrile heroics. "Cristofer Colombo: A Comedy of Discovery" mocks the tedious extravagance of James Branch Cabell's fantasy, *Jurgen*. "How Love Came to General Grant," a classic of the genre, is an amused comment on the bad prose, the improbable melodrama, and the simple-minded piety of Harold Bell Wright. Stewart's im-

19

plied criticism is good-humored but relentless throughout.

Both qualities are apparent in Stewart's fourth chapter, "The Courtship of Miles Standish: In the Manner of F. Scott Fitzgerald." The opening passages concentrate on Fitzgerald's shaky erudition:

> It was of some such yellow-haired Priscilla that Homer dreamed when he smote his lyre and chanted "I sing of arms and the man"; it was at the sight of such as she that rare Ben Johnson's Dr. Faustus cried, "Was this the face that launched a thousand ships?" In all ages has such beauty enchanted the minds of men, calling forth in one century the Fiesolian *terza rima of* "Paradise Lost," in another the passionate arias of a dozen Beethoven symphonies.

Later, Stewart pokes fun at the novelist's fascination with petting parties and prose poetry:

> JOHN: It's really awfully funny—but I came here tonight because Miles Standish made me promise this morning to ask you to marry him. Miles is an awfully good egg, really Priscilla.
>
> PRISCILLA: Speak for yourself, John.
>
> (They kiss.)
>
> PRISCILLA: Again.
>
> JOHN: Again—and again. Oh Lord, I'm gone.
>
> (An hour later John leaves. As the door closes behind him Priscilla sinks back into her chair before the fireplace; an hour passes, and she does not move; her aunt returns from the Bradfords' and after a few ineffectual attempts at conversation goes to bed alone; the candles gutter, flicker, and die out; the room is filled with moonlight, softly stealing through the silken skein of sacred silence. Once more the clock chimes forth the hour—the hour of fluted peace, of dead desire and epic love. Oh not for aye, Endymion, mayst thou unfold the purple panoply of priceless years. She sleeps—Priscilla sleeps—and down the palimpsest of age-old passion the lyres of night breathe forth their poignant

praises. She sleeps—eternal Helen—in the moonlight of a
thousand years; immortal symbol of immortal aeons, flower
of the gods transplanted on a foreign shore, infinitely rare,
infinitely erotic.)

A parody by John Abbot Clark, written thirty years later,
reveals a conspicuous difference in tone and intention. I
quote a few memorable lines from Clark's lampoon "The
Love Song of F. Scott Fitzgerald":

> I should have been a pair of shoulder pads
> Scatting across the gridiron, beating Yale.
>
> In the dorm the coeds come and go
> Talking of Michael Arlen, Bow. . . .
>
> And when I was a youngster, prepping at Newman,
> The coach sent me in to play safety,
> And I was frightened. And out I came.
> In one's room with a book, there you feel free.
> I drink, much of the night, and go south in the winter. . . .
>
> I grow old . . . I am knelled . . .
> I shall no longer wear the bottoms of my trousers belled.
> You will see me any evening in the bar. . . .
>
> But at my back from time to time I hear
> The horns of Marmons and the sax's wail, which shall bring
> Scott to Zelda in the spring.
>
> The novel's strand is broken: *The Last Tycoon* is
> Clutched by stronger hands—the Bunny Hug. The tributes
> Cross from East to West, unheard. The readers are departed.
> Huck's river, run softly, till they end my song.
>
> Mrs. Parker comes at noon.
> And then the lighting of the candles
> In the William Wordsworth Room.
> Shantih shantih shantih [1]

[1] Clark, in *American Literature in Parody,* ed. R. P. Falk (New York,
1955), pp. 227-230.

The contrast between these two satirical treatments is both obvious and significant. Stewart mocks the self-conscious romanticism of some of Fitzgerald's early novels and stories. Clark derives his material, as he informs us in a headnote, from Budd Schulberg's *The Disenchanted* and Arthur Mizener's *The Far Side of Paradise*. Stewart assumes his readers' familiarity with Fitzgerald's fiction. Clark writes for an audience that understands the relevance of terms such as "the Bunny Hug," "Mrs. Parker," and "the William Wordsworth Room"—all biographical details of the sort that are precious to the cocktail-party *cognoscenti*. Stewart's comic exercise reveals amusement at Fitzgerald's literary pretensions. Clark's exhibits contempt for the man. How can we account for these differences in emphasis?

The answer is to be sought not only in the personality and taste of Stewart and Clark, but in the perspective each writer adopted, perhaps unconsciously, toward his subject. Clark wrote at a time when the more sensational features of Fitzgerald's reputation had been recently exposed by Mizener and Schulberg. Stewart wrote at a time when Fitzgerald's life had not yet assumed the troubled and erratic course that would be celebrated by later fictionists and biographers.

But there is an even greater divergence in the attitudes these two parodists imply toward Fitzgerald's works—a divergence so pronounced as to invite a moment's reflection. Clark, apparently, never read anything Fitzgerald wrote. Stewart not only knew Fitzgerald's early fiction intimately; he was also on familiar personal terms with the novelist during the composition of *This Side of Paradise*, the work that forms the basis of his parody. Fitzgerald, in fact, sought Stewart's opinion on the novel when it was still in manuscript.

These encounters between Fitzgerald and Stewart in the

summer of 1919, of no great significance in themselves, anticipate the spirit of exchange and stimulation that was to become characteristic of the period in which Fitzgerald flourished. Stewart's "The Courtship of Miles Standish" reflects that spirit; the parodist's good humor, as well as his concentration on Fitzgerald's art, might be seen as a product of the intimate fellowship of the nineteen-twenties, when in Edmund Wilson's words "the practice of letters was a common craft and the belief in its value a common motivation." On the other hand, Clark's profound indifference to Fitzgerald's works in "The Love Song of F. Scott Fitzgerald" reveals his alienation from that spirit and his dissociation from the sympathy which gave it life.

Fitzgerald's literary companionship with Stewart was typical, not only of the time but also of Fitzgerald's lifelong habit of forming close friendships with fellow writers. In addition, the two authors' subsequent involvements with other writers reveal the interconnections that formed the characteristic pattern of the twenties. For example, Stewart accompanied Hemingway to Pamplona in the summer of 1924; and he served as a model for the fictional character Bill Gorton in *The Sun Also Rises*. Fitzgerald met Hemingway in the fall of 1924, was portrayed briefly in Hemingway's satire *The Torrents of Spring* (1926), and advised Hemingway during the composition of *The Sun Also Rises*. Fitzgerald's discovery of Stewart as a character in Hemingway's novel (then in manuscript) probably came as no surprise: Fitzgerald himself had portrayed some of his "literary friends" in his first two novels. Such portrayals, friendly or otherwise, were a prominent feature of the fiction of the period.

But the close relationships among writers of the twenties prompted other activities which are perhaps of greater interest to the literary historian. Established authors were quick to recognize talent and to assist unknowns into print—as witness Sherwod Anderson's efforts on behalf of William Faulkner or Fitzgerald's on behalf of Hemingway. Editors of *avant-garde* magazines and journals offered encouragement to new writers and provided an outlet for the unorthodox, the strange, the experimental in prose and poetry. Authors circulated manuscripts and sought advice from fellow writers and critics. Sometimes this practice had memorable results, as when Ezra Pound subjected T. S. Eliot's *Waste Land* to a series of drastic cuts, or when Gertrude Stein urged Hemingway to eliminate all "bad" description from his prose. In similar but less tangible ways other members of this professional fraternity benefited from mutual criticism, from mutual stimulation, and from discussion and dispute. Hart Crane's association with Waldo Frank, Matthew Josephson, and Gorham Munson, for example, gave Crane a sense of identification with the common interests and important issues of the age, echoes of which found their way into his poetry. Such artistic cross-fertilization was characteristic of the creative process during the decade.

Writers of other periods, of course, have engaged in similar associations and transactions; the literary community or artistic "cluster" is a commonplace of history.[2] But the feeling persists that the literary community of the nineteen-twenties was unique, that it was distinguished from earlier fellowships by its closeness and by the intensity of its activity. "They had more experiences in common than any other generation in American history," Malcolm Cowley accurately observes. *Exile's Return,* which is based on Cowley's

[2] See A. L. Kroeber, *Configurations of Culture Growth* (Berkeley, Calif., 1944). This voluminous study documents what Kroeber calls "the tendency in human culture for successes or highest values to occur close together in relatively brief periods within nations."

own experience, traces some of the typical patterns of the time: childhood in a small town in the Midwest; a university education interrupted by the compelling patriotic impulse of 1917; service with the Armed Forces in Europe; return, restlessness, expatriation—and above all the fascination with literature, the joint projects and manifestoes, the plethora of *avant-garde* magazines, the common dedication among men who shared a profound interest in their craft.

On the other hand, the writers of the twenties formed no school or specific movement; they had no "program," nor did they limit themselves to doctrinaire principles. The American authors of the postwar decade, in fact, consisted of a number of small separate groups and a great many unaffiliated individuals—all of whom participated freely in public feuds and differences of opinion. There were writers who circulated around individual publishing ventures: for example, the *Broom* group, composed of Cowley, Crane, and Josephson; and the staff of *The American Mercury*—Mencken, Nathan, and Angoff—which later suffered a celebrated parting of the ways. There were regional groups like the Southern Agrarians, "intensive and historical," in Allen Tate's words, and "opposed to the eclectics" in the East. There were the New Humanists, who accepted a relatively unified body of opinion, one of the principal features of which was an opposition to modern literature. There were Mencken and his disciples, who repeatedly castigated the New Humanists. There were journalists on all sides who assailed Mencken regularly. And there was Ernest Hemingway.

Hemingway in particular exemplifies the strong current of dissension that ran through the literature of the period. In *The Torrents of Spring* he satirized Sherwood Anderson, who had been an early friend and mentor. A year later he lampooned Mencken in *The Sun Also Rises*. Later, Gertrude

Stein claimed that Hemingway had "killed a great many of his rivals and put them under the sod." Hemingway avowed that he had not; then he proceeded to heap the sod on Gertrude in *Green Hills of Africa*. She herself had opened hostilities with *The Autobiography of Alice B. Toklas*, in which she not only maligned Hemingway, but expressed her contempt for a number of writers and painters of her acquaintance. Her victims were moved to publish *Testimony Against Gertrude Stein*, which denounced the woman who in the early twenties had been the center of an active and admiring community of artists.

These are only a few of the notable literary quarrels of the twenties and early thirties, when sally and retort were prompted by doctrinal disagreements and personal malice alike. Such disputes, however, clearly reveal an aspect of the individuality these writers clung to so fiercely—without which the era would not have been so productive and so various in accomplishment. Cliquishness and uniformity, undeviating mutual praise and agreement were held in low esteem by the more serious artists of the time, some of whom opposed such things on principle. Perhaps the best perspective on writers of the time reveals a community of literary spirits who were argumentative, self-defensive, and mutually critical, but who nonetheless shared similar ideals and underlying convictions.

This basic unity of attitude found its way into many essay collections and symposiums. By far the most famous of these, *Civilization in the United States* (New York, 1922), suggests the close harmony of opinion among intellectuals and artists on the subject of American culture. Harold Stearns (who also crops up in *The Sun Also Rises*) edited the collection and contributed a grim essay on "The Intellectual Life." Conrad Aiken lamented the plight of the

American poet. J. E. Spingarn decried the fear of personality and intellect in the universities. H. L. Mencken, in a brief survey of American politics, blasted away at the ignorance and dishonesty of our officeholders. Lewis Mumford depicted the horrors of modern industrialization in our cities. Ring Lardner called attention to the "asininity" of American sports spectators. Van Wyck Brooks commented unhappily on "The Literary Life": "The chronic state of our literature," he observed, "is that of a youthful promise which is never redeemed." In his Preface, Stearns summed up one of the basic attitudes which pervaded the entire collection: "the most moving and pathetic fact in the social life of America today is emotional and aesthetic starvation. . . ." Stearns also declared that the volume attempted an "uncompromising analysis" of numerous aspects of American life; only religion had been omitted from the general indictment. "It has been next to impossible to get any one to write on the subject," Stearns confessed. Five years later Sinclair Lewis published *Elmer Gantry,* thereby contributing a powerful supplement to Stearns's symposium and correcting its most notable deficiency.

Civilization in the United States represents the writers and thinkers of the time in one of their most solemn and pessimistic moods. Other essay collections crystallize the spirit of informality characteristic of their lighter moments. Ernest Boyd's *Portraits: Real and Imaginary* (New York, 1924), for example, emphasizes the "private lives" of a number of the author's acquaintances. Satirical in tone and gossipy in content, Boyd's accounts seem trifling and insubstantial to readers of a later generation. The section on Zelda and Scott Fitzgerald is typical:

> . . . with the impunity of their years, they can realize to the
> full all that the Jazz Age has to offer, yet appear as fresh

and innocent and unspoiled as characters in the idyllic world of pure romance. The wicked uncle, Success, has tried to lead these Babes in the Wood away and lose them, but they are always found peacefully sleeping in each other's arms. The kind fairies have watched over them. . . .

And so on. Yet *Portraits: Real and Imaginary* is not altogether insignificant to students of the period: a famous book in its day, it documents the interest writers displayed in the activities, trivial and otherwise, of their contemporaries.

It is also worth noting that one of the portraits in Boyd's gallery, "Aesthete: Model 1924," has a relevance of its own. The international dilettante and literary hanger-on that Boyd depicted was a familiar figure of the age, and he caught the attention of other observers. Fitzgerald's Albert McKiscoe in *Tender Is the Night* and Hemingway's Robert Cohn in *The Sun Also Rises* are specimens of the type. These parallels suggest the accuracy of Boyd's caricature and its pertinence to the era. "Aesthete: Model 1924," in fact, provoked a passionate response from the writers who presumed themselves targets of Boyd's irony; innocuous as the essay may seem today, it was serious business to the literary community that received it.[3]

Another collection, published the same year as Boyd's *Portraits,* presents a picture of that community exchanging banter, mild insults, and mutual approval. *The Literary Spotlight,* edited by John Farrar, is an outstanding instance of group solidarity and chumminess. Farrar's book contains a number of portraits, written by anonymous contributors, of popular literary figures of the day. Each of the essays follows a similar pattern: the subject of discussion is first satirized, then commended. The contributors spar with each

[3] For a detailed version of the story, see Malcolm Cowley, *Exile's Return* (New York, 1956), pp. 190-196.

other without intent to injure; they praise with faint damns. Sherwood Anderson is taken to task for his vanity, but it turns out that his vanity is his great and redeeming virtue. Mencken is pictured as a cruel practical joker, a hypochondriac, and a secret defender of the icons he smashes publicly; still, he is "warmly human" and "a gentleman." Fitzgerald is accused of ignorance and illiteracy, but his genius shines through in *This Side of Paradise*. Similar treatments are accorded Heywood Broun, Sinclair Lewis, Amy Lowell, Floyd Dell, and others. *The Literary Spotlight* is an amiable book, and it exhibits the literary fellowship of the nineteen-twenties in one of its characteristic moments of intimacy.

These, then, were some of the general group characteristics of the writers of the decade. Despite their frequent quarrels and their tendency to fall into separate factions, they were united by a background of similar experience and an intense dedication to the practice of literature. The fact that they were interested in each other, to a greater extent than any other generation of writers before or since, is by no means an incidental or peripheral matter. Out of that interest developed a habit of interchange and mutual influence that does much to explain the affinities in the individual works they produced.

There is no "key" to an understanding of the literature of the nineteen-twenties. Anyone attempting to reduce it to a single essential "formula" courts the error of oversimplification. Yet there are large areas in the works of Fitzgerald and his contemporaries that reveal a fundamental agreement of interest and approach. These writers seem particularly in accord in their selection of themes and their attitudes toward literary technique.

Critics have noted the marked tendency toward technical innovation and experimentation during the twenties.[4] The poetry of Hart Crane, E. E. Cummings, and T. S. Eliot suggests one manifestation of their artistic unorthodoxy. The drama of Eugene O'Neill suggests another. And the art of prose fiction constitutes still another—perhaps the most conspicuous area of improvisation and originality. Fitzgerald's *This Side of Paradise*, Hemingway's *In Our Time* and *The Sun Also Rises*, James Branch Cabell's *Jurgen*, Faulkner's *The Sound and the Fury*, John Dos Passos' *Three Soldiers* and *Manhattan Transfer*—to cite only a few of the most important examples—suggest the variety and range of interest during the postwar decade in new forms of artistic expression.

The writers of the period were united, moreover, in their approach to their sources of literary material: they stressed the importance of the immediate personal experience as a basis for art. Invention, of course, was still important; but the rendering of the actual, the concrete, the observed phenomena of life was given new emphasis. "It was, in fact, an age of indirect or direct 'transcription,'" writes Carlos Baker, "when the perfectly sound aesthetic theory was that the author must invent out of his own experience or run the risk of making hollow men out of his characters." The consistency with which the writers of the twenties and early thirties adopted this theory gives the literature they produced its intense documentary flavor and accounts for its many *romans à clef*. The serious authors of the time felt that they had first to see for themselves before starting to work; they spared no effort to achieve a verisimilitude based on experienced, rather than imagined, reality. Sinclair Lewis did not hesitate to "research" a subject before committing it

[4] The fullest and best treatment is in Frederick J. Hoffman, *The Twenties* (New York, 1955), pp. 163-239.

to novelistic form. Thomas Wolfe relied upon an amazingly profuse store of remembered events and conversations. Fitzgerald used his own experiences at Princeton, his acute observation of the campus, the classrooms, and the conversations of his classmates, in the preparation of *This Side of Paradise*. For *The Sun Also Rises* Ernest Hemingway drew on his recollections of "the way it was" in Pamplona during the summer festival of 1924. How closely Hemingway patterned his first novel on the actual events of that occasion may be seen in Harold Loeb's account, *The Way It Was* (Loeb was the model for Robert Cohn), or in a comment made by Donald Ogden Stewart: ". . . I didn't like the book, for the curious reason that it wasn't a 'novel.' Every damn thing in it was just 'reporting'—at least, up to the end of the fiesta." Stewart might well have underestimated the importance of Hemingway's imaginative presentation of his materials. But works such as Cummings' *Enormous Room* and Dos Passos' *Three Soldiers*—as well as those already mentioned—support the idea that the writers of the nineteen-twenties favored, to a greater extent than previous generations, a background of actual people and events to give their fiction substance and authenticity. Fitzgerald and his contemporaries reversed the doctrine of Shakespeare's Theseus and started, rather than ended, with "a local habitation and a name."

They drew their themes, in the same spirit, from the life around them. The writers of the twenties and early thirties were realists in this respect, too: each recorded with remarkable fidelity the issues and events—as well as the developing, ever-changing attitudes—of his time and place. There are, however, no simple patterns of agreement here. Fitzgerald, Lardner, and Dos Passos, for example, all contributed treatments of the Younger Generation: but each one differs in its perspective. Fitzgerald was the chief his-

torian of the emergent debutantes and playboys, and much
of his early fiction is devoted to a romantic portrayal of their
adventures. Lardner, as we shall see in a later chapter,
made the same group targets of his satire. Dos Passos drew
a picture of the flapper and her escort that emphasizes still
another aspect of the subject: the girl is mildly insane and
the boy is ignorant and self-interested. The reader discovers
variety rather than uniformity in these treatments of a
prominent theme of the twenties. Still, there is agreement
in this instance—and in many others—in the writers' selection of subjects and materials to be treated in fiction.

Furthermore, many authors not only elected the same subjects, but shared similar attitudes toward them. They were
particularly unified in their outspoken, sometimes vehement
reaction against the popular aspirations and values of the
American majority. "Never in history," remarked one of the
most famous critics of the period, "did a literary generation
so revile its country." Perhaps "revile" is too strong a word;
but it is certain that many novelists and short-story writers
turned out cynical interpretations of our habits and attitudes. We might consider, for example, fictional treatments
of village life in the United States. President Harding had
expressed an opinion on the subject that may be taken as
representative of the popular sentiment: "What is the greatest thing in life, my countrymen? Happiness. And there is
more happiness in the American village than in any other
place on earth." Sherwood Anderson did not agree, as is
demonstrated by *Winesburg, Ohio* (1919); neither did
Sinclair Lewis in *Main Street* (1920), Ring Lardner in
"Haircut" (1925), Herbert Asbury in "Hatrack" (1925), or
the Lynds in their documentary study, *Middletown* (1929).

A number of authors also turned their attention to the
automobile, a commodity that had begun to assume signifi-

cant proportions in the life of the average American citizen. Sinclair Lewis showed Babbitt's childish dependence on his motorcar for social status and self-esteem. Faulkner, in *Sartoris*, made the automobile a symbol of the returned veteran's reckless and futile quest for speed and excitement; indeed, for the hero of this Faulkner novel the motorcar is a means of escape from life in a peace-torn world. Other writers extended Faulkner's implication: in Lardner's "There Are Smiles," in Fitzgerald's *The Great Gatsby*, and in Dos Passos' *The Big Money*, the automobile is an instrument of death. Such treatments reflect not only the tremendous increase in production and purchase of automobiles during the twenties, but also the tendency toward machine worship in the public imagination of the time.

In other areas Fitzgerald, Mencken, and Dreiser protested Puritanism and "Comstockery." These same writers, along with Dos Passos and Hemingway, rejected the high-sounding slogans of World War I propaganda. On occasion writers even adopted the same imagery: Faulkner (in *Soldier's Pay*), Fitzgerald (in *The Great Gatsby*), and Hemingway (in *The Sun Also Rises*) all owed a profound debt to the sterile landscape of Eliot's *Waste Land*, one of the most influential depictions of twentieth-century society. These examples, which could easily be multiplied, illustrate the close communion of attitude shared by many of the major writers of the time; but they also suggest, as does the consistent emphasis upon experimental technique, the rebellious tendency of their fiction.

Rebellious they were, certainly, and critical of native mores, of which they were perceptive students. Many aspects of the "rebellion" have been recorded; yet the term is misleading if it creates an image of a spontaneous indictment of American institutions and customs. Taken as a whole, this body of fiction is emphatic in its iconoclasm and its vigorous assault on our weaknesses and illusions. But the same strain is evident in the works of earlier writers. In all periods of its relatively short history, in fact, American literature exhibits a rich vein of social satire and social criticism. Especially prominent since the Civil War, the theme of social criticism may be traced from the beginnings of our tradition to the present, from Hugh Brackenridge to Jack Kerouac. The fiction of the twenties differs, of course, in historical particulars; but it is still very much a traditional body of work in its preoccupations and its philosophy: it is part of the continuity of American letters rather than an isolated episode in its development.

We might accurately call their fundamental theme Democracy in America, after Tocqueville's keen and detached study of our society. The subject is dramatic and multifarious, and it was given particular relevance in the nineteen-twenties by the social and economic forces operating during the postwar era. At no other time in our history have the potential misfortunes of equalitarianism seemed so conspicuous and so close to realization. Brackenridge had observed some of these unwholesome tendencies during the first twenty years of the republic. In his conclusion to *Modern Chivalry* he states that the great moral of his book is "the evil of men seeking office for which they are not qualified." This assertion has familiar echoes to readers of H. L. Mencken, whose era provided abundant material for a similar "great moral" ("I am not fit for this office and should never have been here," confessed Warren Gamaliel Harding). Nineteenth-century writers as diverse as Nathaniel Hawthorne, Mark Twain, and Henry James had focused disillusioned eyes on the subject of the American "aristocracy"; the same theme occupies a prominent position in the works of Lardner, Mencken, Lewis, and Scott Fitzgerald.

In the eighteen-thirties Alexis de Tocqueville had mapped the contours of our culture that would engage native writers almost a century later. Tocqueville saw clearly the rationale of self-interest that dominated American business and the fluidity of movement that characterized our social structure:

> It is strange to see with what feverish ardor the Americans pursue their own welfare and to watch the vague dread that constantly torments them lest they should not have chosen the shortest path which may lead to it. . . . A native of the United States clings to this world's goods as if he were certain never to die: and he is so hasty in grasping at all within reach that one would suppose he was constantly afraid of not living long enough to enjoy them. . . . If in addition to the taste for physical well-being a social condition be added in which neither laws nor customs retain any person in his place, there is a great additional stimulant to this restlessness of temper. Men change their track for fear of missing the shortest cut to happiness.

Tocqueville's comments on national pursuits and motives might easily be applied to the post-World War I period. The spirit of our commercial enterprise during those years of unprecedented prosperity was based in large measure upon the practice and principle of "grasping at all within reach" and a "clinging to this world's goods." The social aspirations of the aggressive middle class (in Tocqueville's telling phrase "the many men restless in the midst of abundance") were recorded time after time by the writers of the nineteen-twenties. These tendencies of democracy in America claimed the attention of Fitzgerald and his contemporaries, as they had attracted the notice of the astute European visitor to our shores almost a century earlier.

The writers of the twenties saw numerous possibilities for variation in these dominant motifs: they contained tragic implications, as in Dreiser's *American Tragedy;* they provided material for comedy, invective, and satire—as in Lardner, Mencken, and Sinclair Lewis; they inspired the powerful sagas of social displacement by William Faulkner; they gave authority and universality to the fictional autobiographies of Thomas Wolfe; and they were the backdrop for the melancholy romances of Scott Fitzgerald.

Whence the emphasis in the novels and stories of the nineteen-twenties upon the social milieu, the pronounced interest in the aspirations of the different classes, in their motives and values? The fiction of the time only directs our attention back to the time itself; and both yield fruitfully to analysis when we understand the process, well known to cultural historians, whereby a literature reflects an age and simultaneously helps to shape it. If we add, further, the forces that work upon the writer's imagination to shape his art, our comprehension of the cycle approaches a state of fullness, however imperfect or incomplete in an absolute sense. In the twenties, few authors worked in isolation. The majority were "involved" in two ways: with the issues and events of the life around them, and with the ideas and attitudes of other contemporary writers. But a specific example at this point will help to clarify the process by which one fictionist of the era derived from his reading the materials of his art, and how those materials crystallize brilliantly an episode in actual national experience. An example appropriate to the purpose is the image of T. J. Eckleburg in Scott Fitzgerald's novel *The Great Gatsby.*

Eckleburg is introduced early in the novel, in the section describing the "valley of ashes" that serves as a Waste Land backdrop for some of the book's crucial action. This bleak area, actually a dumping ground just outside Manhattan, is dominated by a large billboard showing two enormous eyes wearing spectacles and captioned "Doctor T. J. Eckleburg." Presumably this is an optometrist's advertisement placed among the ash heaps to attract the notice of passing commuters. But Fitzgerald suggests that Eckleburg's brooding presence has a larger significance, that the gigantic eyes symbolize some implacable modern deity. Across the road from the desolate valley of ashes lives George Wilson, the spiritless garage owner whose wife, Myrtle, is having an adulterous affair with Tom Buchanan, the unscrupulous and well-to-do representative of Fitzgerald's American "aristocracy" in *The Great Gatsby*. Later, after Myrtle Wilson's death (which occurs in the neighborhood of the dumping ground), George Wilson entertains a curious delusion:

> Wilson's glazed eyes turned out to the ashheaps, where small gray clouds took on fantastic shapes and scurried here and there in the faint dawn wind.
>
> "I spoke to her," he muttered after a long silence. "I told her she might fool me but she couldn't fool God. I took her to the window"—with an effort he got up and walked to the rear window and leaned with his face pressed against it—"and I said 'God knows what you've been doing, everything you've been doing. You may fool me, but you can't fool God!'"
>
> Standing behind him, Michaelis saw with a shock that he was looking at the eyes of Doctor T. J. Eckleburg, which has just emerged, pale and enormous, from the dissolving night.
>
> "God sees everything," repeated Wilson.
>
> "That's an advertisement," Michaelis assured him.

Eckleburg has symbolic reflections elsewhere in the novel; one of Gatsby's party guests reminds us of the optometrist's advertisement: "A stout, middle-aged man, with enormous owl-eyed spectacles. . . ." When we meet this character, who is later referred to as "Owl-Eyes," he is seated in the library musing over Gatsby's books. The amazing thing, Owl-Eyes tells some of the other guests, is that the books are real— "they have pages and everything." Considering the context of Gatsby's world and his papier-mâché palace with its tinsel trappings, Owl-Eyes' surprised discovery is not without relevance. Fitzgerald has extended the implication of Eckleburg's divinity and applied it to Owl-Eyes, one of the few characters in the novel who can distinguish between the apparent and the real.

It should be noted, not incidentally, that Owl-Eyes is the only attendant, aside from Gatsby's father and Nick Carraway, at Gatsby's funeral. And it is he who utters a Jazz Age benediction of sympathy over Gatsby's grave:

> He took off his glasses and wiped them again, outside and in.
> "The poor son-of-a-bitch," he said.

The image of T. J. Eckleburg—as well as his counterpart, Owl-Eyes—has an important function in the over-all rationale of Fitzgerald's novel, and is properly seen as one of its central symbols. The optometrist's advertisement suggests the degenerate state of religious belief in the modern society Fitzgerald is depicting. The image—"God is a billboard"—is appropriate to the morality of self-interest that animates most of the major characters in the novel. Eckleburg broods, not only over the valley of ashes with its quasi-human figures and fantastic shapes, but also over the actions of Tom and Daisy Buchanan, Jordan Baker, and George and Myrtle Wilson—each of whom, in his own way, demonstrates an indifference to ethical standards of conduct. In these respects, Eckleburg is pervasive, integral and significant—an organic part of the intricate metaphorical texture of *The Great Gatsby*.

But the eyes of Doctor Eckleburg constitute more than an effective poetic image; they are also a strikingly accurate distillation of history. In the symbolic representation of God as an advertisement, Fitzgerald documented the peculiarly American, peculiarly modern association of business and religion. Frederick Lewis Allen, in his book *Only Yesterday,* gives us a vivid and detailed summary of the situation that engaged Fitzgerald in *The Great Gatsby*. The association of business with religion, says Allen, was an obvious and important feature of the postwar decade. An annual convention of businessmen in New York City gathered for a three-hour service in the Cathedral of St. John the Divine, Allen tells us; and a famous clergyman of the day lectured them on "Religion in Business." Other sermons in a similar vein were addressed to members of the Advertising Club in a large Eastern city. Many American churches soon formed publicity and advertising departments to help spread the faith through the radio and newspaper media. A national insurance company issued a pamphlet called *Moses, Persuader of Men,* in which the great Hebrew lawgiver was referred to as one of the best salesmen and real-estate promoters in history; a "Fearless, Successful Personality" was Moses, the man who conducted the most magnificent selling campaign of all time. Then there was the famous best-seller of the period, *The Man Nobody Knows,* by Bruce Barton—in which Jesus Christ is portrayed as "the most popular dinner guest in Jerusalem" and "an outdoor man." Christ's disciples were seen as a great executive staff; Christ's parables were the most powerful advertisements in history; and Christ himself was "the founder of modern business." Thus reads the practical theology of the nineteen-twenties.

Fitzgerald was not the only writer of the period to comment critically on the business-of-religion phenomenon; Chapter XVII of Sinclair Lewis's *Babbitt* describes George Babbitt's campaign to "revitalize" the Sunday school of his parish church—according to the best sales methods and modern public-relations procedure. The same theme is touched upon earlier in the novel by the appearance of Mike Munday, the Prophet with a Punch, "the world's greatest salesman of salvation." In a later novel, *Elmer Gantry*, Lewis has the Reverend Gantry cultivate the good will of Zenith newspapermen, who later provide free advertising for his program of salvation. Walter Lippmann, in *A Preface to Morals*, observed sadly that "the modern emancipated man" no longer believes the words of the Gospel: instead, he "believes the best advertised notion." In illustration, Lippmann cited the case of a New York church that sold investment bonds with an interest rate of five per cent; this was to be "an investment in your fellowman's Salvation," and the church proclaimed itself a combination of "Religion and Revenue."

The business-of-religion was paralleled by the development of the religion of business, which became a powerful factor in everyday commercial transactions during Coolidge's administration. "The man who builds a factory," Coolidge himself contended, "builds a temple. . . . The man who works there worships there." John Dos Passos took note of this aspect of American prosperity in a key passage in Volume III of *U.S.A.* Margo Dowling is impressed by the religious atmosphere of her stockbroker's office:

> It always affected Margo a little like church, the whispers, the deferential manners, the boys quick and attentive at the long blackboards marked with columns of symbols, the click

of the telegraph, the firm voice reading the quotations off the ticker at a desk in the back of the room. . . .

In 1926, from the very heart of the prosperity era, R. H. Tawney commented at length on the "new and clamorous economics of the day" and their influence on religion and traditional morality.

All these comments have some relationship to Fitzgerald's rendering of the religion-business theme in the Eckleburg symbol of *The Great Gatsby*. But there is a more specific connection between that image and the essay on advertising by J. Thorne Smith in *Civilization in the United States*. Smith protested against the pervasiveness of this new national industry and the "false and unhealthy" appeal it was exercising on the American public. "Do I understand you to say," asked Smith, "that you do not believe in advertising? Indeed! Soon you will be telling me that you do not believe in God!" To many observers of the mores of the Harding-Coolidge era, this was no irrelevant or merely playful association of ideas. Smith's question, rather, suggested the larger religious and economic patterns of the period. The informed reader will recognize in Fitzgerald's synecdoche a compelling poetic reference to those patterns and their relevance to our behavior.

Thus the Eckleburg image in *The Great Gatsby* demonstrates Fitzgerald's deep understanding of one aspect of modern America and his skill at embodying contemporary attitudes. Eckleburg also reflects Fitzgerald's awareness of what was being written by other perceptive authors of the day. At the same time, the comments on the business-religion phenomenon that occur after the composition of *The Great Gatsby* (those I have cited from Dos Passos and Lippmann, for example) indicate the importance of the subject and the attention it was given by articulate men throughout the period.

From these sources—from his observation of the life of his time and his reading in the works of contemporary fictionists and essayists—Fitzgerald derived a major share of his inspiration. Later chapters, which examine Fitzgerald's relations with Mencken, Lardner, and Hemingway, will confirm this impression. But let us first consider Fitzgerald's long association with Edmund Wilson.

CHAPTER II

Edmund Wilson

> "Believe me, Bunny, it meant more to me
> than it could possibly have meant to you
> to see you that evening. It seemed to renew
> old times. . . ."   —FITZGERALD TO WILSON

Mencken, Lardner, and Hemingway left strong impressions on Fitzgerald's imagination during specific stages of his career. Yet their influence was passing. Wilson's endured. From the beginning he offered Fitzgerald guidance and encouragement, and he did much to infuse into the fledgling novelist a feeling of self-confidence and assurance. Later, he provided professional counsel that significantly affected the course of Fitzgerald's development. Finally, after Fitzgerald's death Wilson became unofficial custodian of his friend's reputation and defender of Fitzgerald's claim to posthumous recognition. Such, briefly stated, were Wilson's contributions to Scott Fitzgerald's literary achievement. That achievement would certainly have been different— and possibly of a lesser order—had it not been for the

Wilson-Fitzgerald companionship, which had its beginning on the tree-shaded campus of Princeton just before World War I.

Fitzgerald came to Princeton full of extracurricular and social ambitions. Christian Gauss, at the time professor of languages and literature and a keen observer of the undergraduates who drew his attention, recalled years later the young Fitzgerald's fascination with the "operatic pageantry" of prewar Princeton and his intense longing to be a Big Man on Campus. The most important part of Fitzgerald's program, it seems, was to become a popular figure, a football hero, and a member of the most prestigious eating club on Prospect Street. These are understandable aspirations in a seventeen-year-old boy from St. Paul, Minnesota. And Princeton, with its numerous extracurricular activities and opportunities for social enrichment, seemed admirably suited to the purpose. Years later, Edmund Wilson expressed regret for the emphasis on "country-house social prestige" that Princeton inspired in the minds of its undergraduates. He felt that Fitzgerald had to some extent fallen victim to the attraction of such nonacademic distinctions.

Yet Fitzgerald's experience as a college student was to be quite different from what he had hoped for—and far more rewarding. He found at Princeton an animated circle of young men absorbed in the study of modern literature and earnestly engaged in developing their talents as writers. Fitzgerald's interest in writing and his awareness of his own lack of sophistication drew him to this group. Although his own knowledge of literature was extremely limited, he had an abiding taste for undergraduate discussions of art and aesthetics, and he participated spiritedly in the sessions presided over by Gauss. The young Midwesterner apparently sensed his own inadequacies as a man of culture; and it was this feeling that first prompted him to seek the company of the more confident John Peale Bishop and Edmund Wilson.

Later on, Fitzgerald and his friends—T. K. Whipple, Wilson, Bishop, and John Biggs—did frequent duty, both as editors and contributors, for the Princeton undergraduate publications. They also wrote for the Triangle Club and acted in its productions. Aside from their parts in these activities, they took the same courses together, held numerous dormitory bull sessions, and before long attracted the attention of fellow students and faculty members alike, who recognized them as a gifted and energetic group, self-sufficient, talented, and marked for distinction.

From the evidence of what they produced during those years, it is clear that they also gained valuable experience. Courses in creative writing were then unknown; Fitzgerald and his comrades learned by practice, and they constantly revived themselves at the fount of their own enthusiasm and mutual interest. At the same time, whatever they achieved on the campus had nothing to do with family connections or membership in one of the miniature Princeton country clubs. Instead, admission to this select fraternity was based on ability. "Exceptional talent must create its own public at Princeton," Fitzgerald once commented, "as it must in life." Fitzgerald and his college chums had been caught up in the spirit that heralded the intense vitality of the productive twenties. Princeton was only one among several Eastern campuses during this period that witnessed a quickening of literary activity, a revived buzz and hum of animation that predicted the extraordinary creativity of the approaching decade.

Wilson had been associated with the *Nassau Lit* from the time of his first year at Princeton (1912-1913). During the early months of Fitzgerald's sophomore year, Wilson, then a junior, urged his friend to submit manuscripts to the magazine. Shortly afterwards Fitzgerald showed Wilson "Shadow Laurels" (a play) and "The Ordeal" (a story). Wilson published both of these in the *Lit* for April and June of that year (1915). Before their appearance Wilson had corrected his friend's faulty spelling and punctuation and, in Wilson's term, "trimmed" his phrases. This encouragement and interest on Wilson's part had important results. Initial publication in Princeton's literary magazine was a decisive step in Fitzgerald's career as a writer, for it marked an important stage in his transition from amateur to professional.

This transition extended over a period of eight or nine years, starting in Fitzgerald's childhood in St. Paul and culminating in Scribner's decision to publish *This Side of Paradise*. Fitzgerald, it is clear, had a strong literary inclination from an early age: he wrote scripts for a number of home-town theatricals and contributed stories to prep-school magazines, on one of which he served as associate editor. These facts immediately dispel the notion that Wilson—or anyone else—started Fitzgerald on his way toward becoming a writer. No such claim is made here. But Wilson did start his friend on a course that proved valuable and that would carry Fitzgerald (as the novelist later remarked) "full swing into my career." For one thing, association with Wilson, both professional and social, gave Fitzgerald a sense of participation in an intellectual and literary milieu. A letter Fitzgerald wrote shortly after he left Princeton suggests his feeling of close affinity with the group of undergraduates who clustered around the *Lit:* "So the short, swift chain of the Princeton intellectuals, Brooke's [1] clothes, clean ears and withall, a lack of mental prigishness . . . Whipple,

---

[1] Fitzgerald's spelling is preserved in all quotations in this and subsequent chapters.

Wilson, Bishop, Fitzgerald . . . have passed along the path of the generation. . . ."

Secondly, Fitzgerald's publications in the college magazine, which continued after Wilson had left Princeton, attracted critical and popular attention of the kind usually accorded a professional writer. As early as 1917, Katherine Fullerton Brush and William Rose Benét wrote critical reviews in the *Daily Princetonian* praising Fitzgerald's work for the *Lit*. At the same time, editors who served on undergraduate publications in other Eastern colleges were mentioning Fitzgerald in their columns as a writer of talent and promise.[2]

Finally, Fitzgerald used much of the material written for the *Lit* in later magazine stories and in sections of *This Side of Paradise*. "The Ordeal," originally accepted by Wilson, appeared in revised form as part of "Benediction," a story published in *The Smart Set* and later included in *Flappers and Philosophers*. Later *Lit* stories and plays, written under the editorships of Bishop and John Biggs, underwent similar transmutation and progress. "The Debutante" and "Babes in the Woods," done for the *Lit* in 1917, were reprinted in *The Smart Set* two years later. "Tarquin of Cheepside" [*sic*], which appeared in the college magazine in 1917, was revised for *The Smart Set* in 1921 and was included in the collection *Tales of the Jazz Age* in 1922. "The Spire and the Gargoyle," *Nassau Lit,* 1917, was later incorporated into *This Side of Paradise,* as were "Babes in the Woods" and "The Debutante."

As an undergraduate, then, Fitzgerald entered into a kind of literary activity that gradually developed into the

[2] For this information I am indebted to an unpublished doctoral dissertation (University of Pennsylvania, 1950) by Henry Dan Piper, "Scott Fitzgerald and the Origins of the Jazz Age."

early stages of his career as a professional writer. Wilson's
part in this crucial transition period should not be underestimated; it was Bishop who initiated Fitzgerald into the
college writing community, but it was Wilson who confirmed his position as an active, contributing member.

Fitzgerald's creative efforts at Princeton were not confined to the *Nassau Lit*. In addition to his activities on the
editorial staff of the *Tiger*—to which he had been elected in
his junior year—he also contributed lyrics and some of the
dialogue for two musicals produced by the Triangle Club.
On one of these, *The Evil Eye*, he collaborated with Wilson.
"I am sick of it myself," Wilson wrote Fitzgerald during an
early stage of its composition. "Perhaps you can infuse into
it some of the fresh effervescence of youth for which you
are so justly celebrated."

Wilson wrote in another vein after Fitzgerald had received
news (in 1916) of his academic failure. Together with
Bishop, Wilson produced for the *Lit* a free-verse summary
of Fitzgerald's years at college:

> I was always clever enough
> To make the clever upperclassmen notice me;
> I could make one poem by Browning,
> One play by Shaw,
> And part of a novel by Meredith
> Go further than most people
> Could do with the reading of years;
> And I could always be cynically amusing at the expense
> Of those who were cleverer than I
> And from whom I borrowed freely,
> But whose cleverness
> Was not the kind that is effective
> In the February of sophomore year. . . .
> No doubt by senior year
> I would have been on every committee in college,

But I made one slip:
I flunked out in the middle of junior year.

The Wilson-Bishop lampoon climaxed a year that was full
of disappointments for Fitzgerald. His concentration on
extracurricular activities had put him far behind in his
studies; an attack of malaria confined him for long periods
to a bed in the school infirmary. Late in the semester he left
Princeton, partly because of poor health and partly because
he rightly assumed that he was in danger of flunking out at
the end of the term.

But the following September, Fitzgerald was back at
Princeton to begin his junior year over again. Wilson, in the
meantime, had been graduated the previous June and had
set up bachelor quarters on Eighth Street in New York City.
Here Fitzgerald visited him the next winter. "I was still an
undergraduate at Princeton," the novelist wrote fifteen years
later, remembering his afternoon with Wilson, "while he
had become a New Yorker." To Fitzgerald, Wilson had
become "the metropolitan spirit" incarnate—the cosmopolitan literary sophisticate in his natural habitat:

> . . . that night, in Bunny's apartment, life was mellow and
> safe, a finer distillation of all that I had come to love at
> Princeton. The gentle playing of an oboe mingled with city
> noises from the street outside, which penetrated into the
> room with difficulty through great barricades of books. . . .
> I had found a third symbol of New York and I began
> wondering about the rent of such apartments and casting
> about for the appropriate friends to share one with me.

In such ways did Wilson fire Fitzgerald's imagination and
stimulate his ambition to become a man of letters. He was
a friend whose judgment Fitzgerald valued; he helped
establish Fitzgerald firmly in the transitional phase of his

career; he edited and corrected Fitzgerald's manuscripts; he collaborated with Fitzgerald on a literary project; he gave Fitzgerald a taste of active membership in a community of practicing writers; he acted as self-appointed critic of Fitzgerald's attitudes and pretensions; and immediately after his graduation he became a representative figure: he epitomized all that was admirable in the cultured, self-assured gentleman-writer—an image that Fitzgerald, as we shall see presently, attempted to emulate. These are formative elements in the Wilson-Fitzgerald relationship that look forward to the mature association of later years, when Wilson played an important part in Fitzgerald's development as a disciplined craftsman and literary stylist.

It should be understood, however, that Wilson did not occupy a position of pre-eminence among the many friends Fitzgerald made at Princeton. The latter's admiration for men such as Father Fay, Shane Leslie, John Peale Bishop, and Henry Strater was as considerable; and their impact on *This Side of Paradise* was more immediate. From each of these companions Fitzgerald learned valuable lessons, though he never became a "disciple" of any one of them— including Wilson. There was nothing slavish or over-dependent in any of his friendships.

Still, Wilson remained an undeniable force in Fitzgerald's life. Shortly after leaving college, both men served in the Armed Forces—Fitzgerald as an infantry lieutenant stationed in various Army camps in the South and Midwest, and Wilson as a sergeant with the A.E.F. in France. Separated as they were, they exchanged frequent letters that contained news of their own current literary projects and those of close friends. Fitzgerald was devoting off-duty weekends to a novel he had begun before leaving Princeton. Early in 1918 he sent Wilson a description of this work in progress, including a tentative title page:

THE ROMANTIC EGOTIST
by F. Scott Fitzgerald
CHAS. SCRIBNER'S SONS (MAYBE!)
MCMXVIII

This is a reference to an early version of *This Side of Paradise*.

Fitzgerald was discharged from military service in February, 1919. Soon afterwards he established himself in New York; he was in earnest now about becoming a writer; he would try his hand in the literary capital. But instead of the immediate success he had envisioned, he encountered only frustration and disappointment. His ambition of the moment was to work for one of the metropolitan newspapers; he hoped to "trail murderers by day and write short stories by night." But no newspaper would hire him, and his stories were rejected, one after another, by the magazines. He took a job with an advertising agency, writing slogans for obscure commercial enterprises in which he had no interest. And he decorated the walls of his room in upper Manhattan with one hundred and twenty-two rejection slips.

The impatience of Fitzgerald's fiancée, Zelda Sayre, gave his desire for success additional urgency; she had repeatedly expressed her reluctance to marry an advertising clerk who made ninety dollars a month. But although the prospect of losing Zelda added poignancy to his seeming failure that spring, Fitzgerald was equally depressed by the collapse of his dream of becoming a part of "the metropolitan spirit." In an autobiographical essay written in 1932 he recalled the circumstances which interfered with his plan to become a literary gentleman in the style of Edmund Wilson:

When I got back to New York in 1919, I was so entangled in life that a period of mellow monasticism in Washington

Square was not to be dreamed of. The thing was to make enough money in the advertising business to rent a stuffy apartment for two in the Bronx. The girl concerned had never seen New York but she was wise enough to be rather reluctant. And in a haze of anxiety and unhappiness I passed the four most impressionable months of my life.

In his disillusioned frame of mind, Fitzgerald was particularly susceptible to the atmosphere of cynicism which consistently intruded upon his naive and optimistic expectations:

> One by one my great dreams of New York became tainted. The remembered charm of Bunny's apartment faded with the rest when I interviewed a blowsy landlady in Greenwich Village. She told me I could bring girls to my room, and the idea filled me with dismay—why should I want to bring girls to my room?—I had a girl. . . . I was a failure—mediocre at advertising work and unable to get started as a writer. Hating the city, I got roaring, weeping drunk on my last penny and went home. . . .

From this account and others in similar vein, it is obvious that Fitzgerald looked on this period of his life as totally unprofitable. But there was a notable exception to his pattern of failure. Sometime during that spring of 1919 he was introduced to George Jean Nathan, then coeditor with H. L. Mencken of *The Smart Set*. The meeting resulted in Fitzgerald's first story sale to a magazine. In June of that year, before he left for St. Paul, Fitzgerald received thirty dollars from *The Smart Set* for "Babes in the Woods," which had appeared in the *Nassau Lit* in 1917. The encounter with Nathan was a significant point in Fitzgerald's career for other reasons as well: it marked the beginning of his relationship with H. L. Mencken, who was to exert a considerable influence, as we shall see in a later chapter, on the fiction Fitzgerald produced during the early twenties.

Edmund Wilson had arranged the meeting with George Jean Nathan. Wilson and Fitzgerald, along with John Peale Bishop, visited the young editor in his hotel room. It is a scene worth picturing, Fitzgerald's initiation into the professional fellowship. Four young men, each destined for a particular form of distinction in the literary world—Wilson, serious, already self-assured; Bishop, somewhat the elegant dandy; Nathan, racy and cosmopolitan; and Fitzgerald, uncertain but enthusiastic: a plenitude of youth, ideas, and promise. Nathan produced food and wine; he explained that he needed new material; failure to submit plays and stories, he insisted, would be taken as a personal affront. Later, Wilson rewrote a short story under Nathan's direction; but the latter still found it unacceptable. Fitzgerald's "Babes in the Woods" was purchased and eventually published.[3]

But at the time neither the thirty dollars nor Nathan's interest could mitigate Fitzgerald's feeling of defeat. He returned to St. Paul and spent the summer reworking his novel. By August he was so deeply engrossed in completing the revision that he could not find time to comply with a request from Wilson, who was collaborating with Stanley Dell on an anthology of tales concerning "America's part in the war." Wilson wanted Fitzgerald to contribute something about Army life in the United States. "Will start on story for you about 25 d'Aout (as the French say or do not say) (which is about 10 days off)," Fitzgerald wrote. But a month later he confessed: "Haven't had time to hit a story for you yet. Better not count on me as the w. of i. or the E. S. are rather dry." This second letter contained the news that Scribner's had decided to publish *This Side of Paradise*.

Wilson had advised Fitzgerald on early drafts of this

[3] William Manchester, *Disturber of the Peace* (New York, 1951), pp. 133-134.

novel, which he had seen in manuscript. In November, two months after it had been accepted for publication, Fitzgerald sent Wilson a copy of the final version. Wilson responded with the same kind of friendly derision he had invoked to commemorate Fitzgerald's failure at Princeton:

> I have just read your novel with more delight than I can well tell you. It ought to be a classic in a class with *The Young Visiters*. . . . Your hero is an unreal imitation of Michael Fane of Sinister Street who was himself unreal. . . . As an intellectual Amory is a fake of the first water and I read his views on art, politics, religion and society with more riotous mirth than I should care to have you know. . . . I was also very much shocked when poor old John Bishop's hair stands up on end at beholding the devil. . . .

But Wilson concluded with a word of praise and some serious advice:

> I don't want to bludgeon you too brutally, however, for I think that some of the poems and descriptions are exceedingly good. It would all be better if you would tighten up your artistic conscience and pay a little more attention to form. . . . I feel called upon to give you this advice because I believe you might become a very popular trashy novelist without much difficulty.

After the book had been released and was enjoying a high degree of success, Wilson wrote an article for *The Bookman* in which he recorded further impressions:

> [*This Side of Paradise*] has almost every fault and deficiency that a novel can possibly have. It is not only highly imitative but it imitates an inferior model. . . . The story itself, furthermore, is very immaturely imagined: it is always verging on the ludicrous. And, finally, *This Side of Paradise* is one of the most illiterate books of any merit ever published. . . . Not only is it ornamented with bogus ideas and

faked literary references, but it is full of literary words tossed about with the most reckless inaccuracy.

But once again Wilson qualified his view of the book's weakness:

> I have said that *This Side of Paradise* commits almost every sin that a novel can possibly commit: but it does not commit the unpardonable sin: it does not fail to live.

Fitzgerald no doubt felt some slight resentment at Wilson's critical comments; in an essay written fifteen years later he remarked with a trace of annoyance not quite forgotten: "A lot of people thought it was a fake, and perhaps it was, and a lot of others thought it was a lie—which it was not." But on another occasion, Fitzgerald expressed a judgment of *This Side of Paradise* that parallels Wilson's very closely. "Looking it over," he wrote Maxwell Perkins in 1938, "I think it is now one of the funniest books since 'Dorian Gray' in its utter spuriousness—and then, here and there, I find a page that is real and living." And to his daughter Fitzgerald wrote a brief criticism of a novel by Thomas Wolfe, in which he concluded, using the same words Wilson had used twenty years earlier: "However, the book doesn't commit the cardinal sin: it doesn't fail to live." Wilson's opinions concerning Fitzgerald's first novel, and others he expressed during the course of his friend's development, left a lasting impression.

Wilson's *Bookman* essay also contained an examination of *The Beautiful and Damned*, which had just been published. "In college," Wilson wrote, "[Fitzgerald] had supposed that the thing to do was to write biographical novels with a burst of ideas toward the close; since his advent in the literary world, he has discovered that another genre has recently come into favor: the kind which makes much of the tragedy and what Mencken has called 'the meaninglessness of life.' Fitzgerald had imagined, hitherto, that the thing to do in a novel was to bring out a meaning in life; but he now set about it to contrive a shattering tragedy that should be, also, a hundred-per-cent meaningless." But in his conclusion Wilson added: "*The Beautiful and Damned,* imperfect though it is, marks an advance over *This Side of Paradise:* the style is more nearly mature and the subject more solidly unified, and there are scenes that are more convincing than any in his previous fiction."

Fitzgerald had worked on *The Beautiful and Damned* during the fall of 1920 and the winter and spring of 1921. Early in 1921, Wilson had seen parts of the novel in manuscript and had strongly urged Fitzgerald to revise certain sections, particularly the "midnight symposium" scene in Book III. Fitzgerald later rewrote the passage and sent the revised version for Wilson's approval. That Wilson still did not think the "symposium" section—or *The Beautiful and Damned* as a whole—artistically satisfactory is clearly indicated in the review I have just quoted, in which Wilson singled out "the meaninglessness of life" theme as the book's principal weakness (the "symposium" chapter emphasizes this theme). Apparently, too, the heavy tone of irony Fitzgerald employed in the novel failed to please Wilson, though he had urged Fitzgerald earlier to view his material for fiction with "cosmic irony."

But Wilson responded enthusiastically to Fitzgerald's next major project. *The Vegetable,* Wilson said in a letter dated May 26, 1922, was "one of the best things" Fitzgerald had written. "Go on writing plays," Wilson recommended; and he added that *The Vegetable* was "the best American comedy ever written." In the same letter Wilson suggested revisions, chiefly structural, which Fitzgerald adopted when he came to rewrite the play.

During the next few months Wilson acted as amateur

agent for Fitzgerald, who was in St. Paul at the time; several letters from Wilson in June and July report progress on the reception of *The Vegetable* by the Theatre Guild and various actors and theatrical producers. Fitzgerald worked on the play all through the summer and well into the fall. The following spring Sam Harris agreed to produce it, and *The Vegetable* opened in Atlantic City in November, 1923. In his dedication to the Scribner's edition of the play Fitzgerald remembered the assistance provided by Wilson over a four- or five-year period:

> To Katherine Tighe and Edmund Wilson, Jr.
> Who Deleted Many Absurdities
> From My First Two Novels I Recommend
> The Absurdities Set Down Here

The Vegetable was a financial failure, and it seems to later readers a totally unsuccessful venture into dramatic art. Yet Wilson's praise is understandable. At the time, he was disturbed by Fitzgerald's apparent inability to present a theme or an extended dramatic action without digressions and irrelevant episodes. In this technical sense *The Vegetable* represents an improvement over *This Side of Paradise* and *The Beautiful and Damned*, for it is more concise than either of the two novels and does not stray as frequently into peripheral or loosely related areas. Then, too, the theme of *The Vegetable*, which dramatizes the absurdity of American politics, might have seemed more vital to a contemporary than it would to most readers today. Forty years after the composition of *The Vegetable* it is clear that Fitzgerald's characters are uniformly uninteresting stereotypes and his treatment of American politics superficial even for the purposes of dramatic farce. But these deficiencies might have been overlooked by a perceptive critic who was preoccupied with problems of technique, and who was bound by close ties to the author and to the era he portrayed. If the passage of time and a more advantageous perspective of Fitzgerald's works have contradicted Wilson's opinion in this instance, they have vindicated him in every other judgment he expressed on the subject of his friend's achievement.

The general soundness of Wilson's critical views is evident, for example, in his reception of *The Great Gatsby*. Wilson not only approved Fitzgerald's third novel; he thought it his finest work up to that time. In 1926, a year after *Gatsby* appeared, Wilson commented in his essay "The All-Star Literary Vaudeville" that Fitzgerald seemed to be entering upon a new course of development; the "vividness" and "glamor" of Fitzgerald's early fiction, Wilson thought, was now being supplemented by the young novelist's "mastery of his material." Two years later Wilson observed that Fitzgerald "had learned very fast as a writer; his ideals for his art had gone rapidly up. Each of his three novels, from the point of view of form and conception, had been a startling improvement on the one before." In 1941, in his Introduction to the Scribner edition of *The Last Tycoon*, Wilson noted: "It is worth while to read *The Great Gatsby* in connection with *The Last Tycoon* because it shows the kind of thing that Fitzgerald was aiming to do in the latter. . . . He had recovered here the singleness of purpose, the sureness of craftsmanship, which appear in the earlier story." In 1952, Wilson wrote a memorial essay on Christian Gauss in which he praised *The Great Gatsby* as an "organized impersonal" novel in which "every word, every cadence, every detail [performed] a definite function in producing an intense effect." It should be added that although later critics have confirmed Wilson's views on the merits of *The Great Gatsby*, contemporary reviewers—among them H. L. Mencken—found the novel unsatisfactory; it was "soft," "artificial," of "negligible" value, some readers thought, and inferior to Fitzgerald's earlier works.

Other critics and writers, of course, had high praise for *The Great Gatsby:* Fitzgerald received letters of commendation from Gertrude Stein, Edith Wharton, and T. S. Eliot. For these opinions, and for Wilson's, Fitzgerald had great respect. No doubt he was influenced by them when, toward the end of his life, he wrote his daughter: "What little I've accomplished has been by the most laborious and uphill work, and I wish now I'd *never* relaxed or looked back— but said at the end of *The Great Gatsby:* 'I've found my line —from now on this comes first. This is my immediate duty— without this I am nothing.'"

There is no evidence that Wilson advised Fitzgerald during the composition of *Gatsby* (Bishop certainly did). But Wilson had recommended the novels of Henry James, which Fitzgerald adopted as guides to style while he was working on *Gatsby;* and Wilson had consistently stressed the idea that Fitzgerald's writing would profit greatly from increased discipline and more careful control of material. Wilson's influence, though indirect, was not insignificant.

Edmund Wilson had an underlying respect for Fitzgerald's endeavors; even his most unfavorable critical comments are tempered by a note of encouragement and approval. And for Fitzgerald's best efforts—or for what Wilson took to be Fitzgerald's best efforts—Wilson had unqualified praise. But on occasion Wilson did not hesitate to adopt the role of a stern tutor with little patience for the tomfoolery of his exuberant student. Certain minor episodes in the course of their relationship bring out this aspect of Wilson's attitude.

In 1924, for example, Fitzgerald supplied the title for a

collection of stories by Ring Lardner. This volume, which contained some of Lardner's most serious work, included a flippant introduction in which Lardner offered the book to the public as a guide to story writing. *How To Write Short Stories* was a great success both critically and financially. The trade publication *Printer's Ink* commended Scribner's on the title and the presentation; it was, said the editors of the magazine, "a new way of putting out a product so as to distinguish it." Others were equally enthusiastic, as Lardner reported to Fitzgerald shortly after the book was published: "Michael Arlen, who is here to watch the staging of The Green Hat, said he thought How To Write Short Stories was a great title for my book and when I told him it was your title, he said he had heard a great deal about you and was sorry to miss you."

Wilson, writing a review for *The Dial*, commented:

Mr. Ring Lardner is a popular journalist who writes for the New York *American* and who also provides the text for a syndicated comic strip. It has therefore been thought appropriate to present his new collection of short stories as if it were a volume of popular humor. There are a preface in the vein of Bill Nye and a jocose introduction to every story, and the title page is brightened by a humorous cut that is evidently by John Held. The book itself, from its burlesque preface, is called *How To Write Short Stories*, instead of, as it ought to be, *Champion and Other Stories*.

Is all this an idea of the publishers, who do not want to forfeit the prestige of Mr. Lardner's reputation as a humorist, or is it due to Mr. Lardner, who is timid about coming forward in the role of serious writer? The fact is that this new book of his, instead of belonging to the gruesome department of, say, Irvin Cobb's *Speaking of Operations*, contains some of the most interesting work that Ring Lardner has yet produced. These stories, he observes in his preface, "will illustrate in a half-hearted way what I am trying to get at." But the stories are not half-hearted: it is the jokes that he intrudes among them.

Wilson knew very well whose idea the title was; one of Fitzgerald's letters, in which the novelist hesitantly tries to assert himself, suggests as much: "you are wrong about Ring's book. My title was the best possible. You are always wrong—but always with the most correct possible reasons. (This statement is merely acrocrytical, hypothetical, diabolical, metaphorical.)"

Nine years later, Fitzgerald received a letter from Bruce Bliven, who was then editor of *The New Republic:* "Edmund Wilson tells me that you know a great deal about Ring Lardner, and that you might be willing to write something about him for us. . . . On the chance that you may not have seen the daily papers, perhaps I ought to say that my telegram and this letter are caused by the fact that Lardner died yesterday."

Fitzgerald did write something: his prose elegy, "Ring," is at once a personal reminiscence, a critical estimate of Lardner's works, and an affectionate tribute to a friend. Fitzgerald's memorial concludes with the passage: "A great and good American is dead. Let us not obscure him by the flowers, but walk up and look at that fine medallion, all abraded by sorrows that perhaps we are not equipped to understand. Ring made no enemies, because he was kind, and to many millions he gave release and delight."

Wilson's reaction to Fitzgerald's essay on Lardner is another illustration of his attitude toward his friend. Other of Fitzgerald's acquaintances were extremely impressed with "Ring." Preserved in Fitzgerald's correspondence files are a number of letters the novelist received soon after "Ring" appeared in *The New Republic.* Dorothy Parker wrote that it was the finest and most moving thing she had ever read. Franklin Adams called it "a loving piece," and confessed that it had made him cry. Maxwell Perkins commented that it was a "very fine piece." Sherwood Anderson wrote, "That was a swell piece you wrote about Ring Lardner." Most lavish in its appreciation was a letter from John O'Hara, who said that if Fitzgerald had never written another line, "Ring" would have been writing career enough for anyone. Only Wilson dissented. "I thought the phrase 'great and good American' sounded like a political speech," he wrote Fitzgerald. "Lardner wasn't great anyway, was he? . . . his chief claim to distinction was a gift for Swiftian satire based on hate."

This undercurrent seems to have flowed steadily through the Wilson-Fitzgerald relationship; Wilson had rapped Fitzgerald's knuckles on other occasions, such as those mentioned earlier in the section on Fitzgerald's years at Princeton. Parts of Wilson's letters to Fitzgerald concerning the defects of his first two novels also seem rather harsh, sounding as they do a note of contempt for the novelist's early efforts. From the beginning, perhaps, Wilson's attitude was tinged with a trace of malice or even, in the case of the Lardner memorial, jealousy. Or is it more accurate to accuse Edmund Wilson of occasional stuffiness? A recent parody in *Punch,* entitled "To the Comfort Station," exhibits Wilson in the act of advising William Shakespeare on "the difference between good and bad art" (Shakespeare has stopped overnight at Princeton to ask Wilson's opinion on his next play, *King Lear*):

> That week had already been a hard one for me [the parody continues], teaching Scott Fitzgerald and Ernest Hemingway how to write, and explaining to them about T. S. Eliot and Henry James, so I may have spoken abruptly when

Mr. Shakespeare did not seem to get my meaning at once. . . .

He did not take my advice and a printed copy of the play now lies before me. . . . I had told him clearly how the flaws in his psychology could be put right. He seems to have done little or nothing to justify my hopes that he would extend his reading. I am beginning to suspect that some writers are not worth helping, or at least that a stop-over in Princeton is not enough for them to absorb all I have to tell them.

There is a third alternative which must be mentioned in these speculations about Wilson's feelings toward Fitzgerald: perhaps Wilson the critic valued honesty above sentiment.

Whatever the underlying emotions, the master-pupil aspect was dominant, and it sometimes produced strain and personal friction. Wilson was aware of this fact when he visited Fitzgerald in 1928. The two friends had seen little of each other during the intervening four years when Fitzgerald had been on extended sojourns in Europe. Now settled, at least temporarily, in an impressive mansion (called "Ellerslie") in Delaware, Fitzgerald sent Wilson an aggressively jolly note of invitation to spend a weekend, along with several other guests, at Ellerslie. Wilson accepted the invitation, but he thought he detected a faint hostility in Fitzgerald's letter, and he had some misgivings about going at all. Wilson believed the relationship had suffered "a certain chill." At the time Fitzgerald was worried about his failure to complete a novel he had already worked on for several years (this eventually became *Tender Is the Night*). The novelist felt touchy about his creative slump, and particularly so when he had to admit it to Wilson, to whom he felt somehow accountable. "It was his own artistic conscience that accused him," Wilson later remarked, "but this was beginning to make our meetings uncomfortable, for any inquiry about his work was likely to bring a sharp retort."

A few years later Fitzgerald visited Wilson in New York —with unhappy results. The novelist was weighed down by an all but crushing volume of professional and personal difficulties: his wife was in a mental institution, he himself was struggling against alcoholism and poor health, and the long anticipated novel was still unfinished. In a mood of "desperate impotence"—the words are Fitzgerald's—he spent an afternoon with Wilson in an atmosphere, as we may well imagine, that was far from agreeable for either party. Afterwards, Fitzgerald sent a note of apology assuming "'full responsibility for all unpleasantness.'"

"What I object to," Wilson replied some months later, "is precisely the 'scholar and vulgarian,' 'you helped me more than I helped you' business. I know that this isn't a role you've foisted on me; I've partly created it myself." The period of dissension, however, ended permanently not long after this exchange. "It was good seeing you again," Fitzgerald wrote early in 1934, "and good to think that our squabble, or whatever it was, is ironed out."

Fitzgerald's "squabble" with Wilson took place around the time of the completion of *Tender Is the Night*, a book that bears little, if any, of Wilson's mark. The causes of this partial eclipse of Wilson's influence are complex: Fitzgerald had lived abroad during much of the time spent writing *Tender Is the Night;* his meetings with Wilson were infrequent, even after he returned to America. He had developed a sensitivity, already noted, to his role as "vulgarian" at the feet of the "scholar." And finally, he was strongly under the influence of Ernest Hemingway when *Tender Is the Night* was in progress.

Yet even here Wilson played a part, though it was indirect. It was he who introduced Fitzgerald to Hemingway's works and urged him to "look up" the obscure young author of *Three Stories and Ten Poems* when Fitzgerald departed for Europe in 1924. Thus Wilson was responsible for inaugurating another important cycle of influence in Fitzgerald's life.

Wilson read *Tender Is the Night* when it appeared in serial form in *Scribner's Magazine* during the early months of 1934. This novel, which had undergone numerous revisions and reconstructions over a nine-year period, Wilson found partially unsatisfactory. In conversation with Fitzgerald he criticized the characterizations in the book; and years later he made the comment: "His conception of his subject in *Tender Is the Night* had shifted in the course of his writing it so that the parts of that fascinating novel do not always quite hang together. . . ."

It was not until after Fitzgerald's death that Wilson again publicly expressed unreserved approval of his friend's abilities as a novelist. In *The Last Tycoon* Wilson saw the unity of structure, the concentration on a single, undeviating line of dramatic development, and the concise forcefulness of phrase which had distinguished *The Great Gatsby*. Wilson had admired "Crazy Sunday," a short story based on Fitzgerald's experiences in the motion-picture capital in 1931. He thought he detected in the Hollywood setting a source of material for an important novel. In a letter written in 1932 (shortly after the appearance of "Crazy Sunday"), Wilson advised: "You should do something more about Hollywood, which anybody who knows anything about is either scared or bribed not to tell about or have convinced themselves is all right."

Several years later Wilson expressed his confidence in Fitzgerald's ability to treat the subject honestly: "I hope [your novel] is about Hollywood—I've read practically all the novels ever written on the subject, and none of them really do much with it." *The Last Tycoon* is evidence of Fitzgerald's intention to portray Hollywood accurately, without false glamor—and a justification of Wilson's confidence. In a letter written to Wilson in November, 1940, Fitzgerald assured his friend, "I think my novel is good. I've written it with difficulty. It is completely upstream in mood and will get a certain amount of abuse but it is first hand and I am trying a little harder than I ever have to be exact and honest emotionally. I honestly hoped somebody else would write it but nobody seems to be going to." A month after he wrote this letter Scott Fitzgerald was dead, and *The Last Tycoon* was interrupted at midpoint in its composition.

Soon afterward Wilson began to exert himself on his friend's behalf, adopting for a time the role of custodian of Fitzgerald's reputation. The obituary notices that appeared in newspapers and magazines indicate that Fitzgerald was considered, at the time of his death, an insignificant minor writer whose works had not survived their period of composition. It is unlikely that this attitude would have prevailed, with or without Edmund Wilson's efforts to correct it. But it is certain that Wilson was to a great extent responsible for the resurgence of interest in Fitzgerald as an important American novelist.

As an initial move in this direction Wilson published a short study of contemporary novelists who at one time or another had used California as a setting for their fiction. This brief survey, which appeared a few months after Fitzgerald's death, concluded with some comments on *The Last Tycoon*:

> Scott Fitzgerald, an accomplished artist, had written a considerable part of what promised to be by all odds the best novel ever devoted to Hollywood. There you are shown the

society and the business of the movies, no longer through the eyes of the visitor to whom everything is glamorous or ridiculous, but from the point of view of people who have grown up or lived with the industry and to whom its values and laws are their natural habit of life. These are criticized by higher standards and in the knowledge of wider horizons, but the criticism is implicit in the story; and in the meantime, Scott Fitzgerald, by putting us inside their group and making us take things for granted, is able to excite an interest in the mixed destiny of his Jewish producer of a kind that lifts the novel quite out of the class of this specialized Hollywood fiction and relates it to the story of man in all times and in all places.

At the time this essay appeared, Wilson was preparing *The Last Tycoon* for publication. He edited the manuscript, collected, arranged, and interpreted Fitzgerald's notes for the unfinished portions of the novel, and wrote an introduction for the volume, which in its final form assumed the proportions of a Fitzgerald "omnibus" (in addition to *The Last Tycoon*, it contained *The Great Gatsby*, "May Day," "The Diamond as Big as the Ritz," "The Rich Boy," "Absolution," and "Crazy Sunday"). Wilson apparently hoped to dispel public apathy by exhibiting, in one volume, almost all of Fitzgerald's best work. In his introduction Wilson wrote:

> *The Last Tycoon* is . . . Fitzgerald's most mature piece of work. . . . The moving-picture business in America has been observed at close range, studied with a careful attention and dramatized with a sharp wit such as are not to be found in combination in any of the other novels on the subject. *The Last Tycoon* is far and away the best novel we have had about Hollywood, and it is the only one which takes us inside. . . . In going through the immense pile of drafts and notes that the author had made for this novel, one is confirmed and reinforced in one's impression that

Fitzgerald will be found to stand out as one of the first-rate figures in the American writing of his period.

American critics and fictionists gave *The Last Tycoon* a memorable reception. John Dos Passos thought Fitzgerald's fragment represented "the beginnings of a great novel." Dos Passos believed Fitzgerald's last effort established the novelist as an artist of the first rank. He also observed, somewhat extravagantly, that the prose of *The Last Tycoon* was of sufficient grandeur and importance to raise the level of subsequent American fiction, much as Marlowe's blank verse had elevated Elizabethan dramatic poetry. James Thurber, writing in *The New Republic*, remarked that *The Last Tycoon* had provoked more discussion among writers and critics than any other book of recent years. Thurber thought Fitzgerald's last work was drawn upon "the largest canvas of his life" and that Fitzgerald would have brought it off "brilliantly," as he had done earlier with *Gatsby*. Stephen Vincent Benét was also impressed: he praised *The Last Tycoon* for its "wit, observation, sure craftsmanship, and verbal felicity." Benét concluded by prophesying that Fitzgerald's reputation would be one of the most enduring of our time.

In the years that followed the publication of *The Last Tycoon*, Wilson made repeated references in his essays to Fitzgerald and his achievement as a writer. This was in no sense a deliberate "campaign"; all allusions to Fitzgerald are integral parts of whatever subject Wilson happened to be discussing. Yet even in the absence of any contriving or calculation, Wilson frequently managed between 1942 and 1945 to lend his own substantial support to the perpetuation of his friend's name.[4]

In 1945, Wilson published *The Crack-Up*. This volume

[4] See, for example, Wilson's essay collection *Classics and Commercials* (New York, 1950), pp. 70, 105, 110, 140, 170.

contains a large sampling of Fitzgerald's correspondence, a number of his autobiographical essays, selections from his notebooks, letters from well-known literary figures, and poems and critical essays about Fitzgerald written by friends and fellow authors. The time and care Wilson devoted to preparing this collection are evident in its scrupulous editing of personal documents and its artful selection and arrangement of material.

The Crack-Up aroused a great deal of interest and excitement among literary commentators. One after another they published essays which praised the volume as a unique record of a writer's personality as well as an intimate revelation of his professional struggles. But many reviewers did not stop there; they used The Crack-Up as a point of departure for surveying Fitzgerald's life and works, and for evaluating his contribution to American fiction. These writers and critics, of course, disagreed on certain particulars. But they were unanimous in their judgment that Fitzgerald deserved critical and popular attention.[5] Wilson was thus responsible for another surge of interest in Scott Fitzgerald, the man and the author.

The publication of The Crack-Up marked the highest point of Fitzgerald's reputation since his early popularity in the twenties. After The Crack-Up, influential critics like Lionel Trilling contributed forcefully to the recognition Fitzgerald was to receive in the nineteen-fifties. Arthur Mizener's biography further impressed the novelist's importance upon thousands of readers, especially on university campuses. The late fifties and early sixties have witnessed a sustained interest in Fitzgerald's life and works, and dra-

[5] See F. Scott Fitzgerald: The Man and His Work (New York, 1951), essays by Malcolm Cowley, Andrews Wanning, Mark Schorer, Alfred Kazin, J. F. Powers, and William Troy, pp. 146-193. Other friends of Fitzgerald, Dorothy Parker and John O'Hara, edited The Viking Portable F. Scott Fitzgerald the same year The Crack-Up appeared.

matically high sales of his books. Wilson's contribution to all this is difficult to assess; but the part he played in recalling Fitzgerald to public and critical attention was obviously significant.

The foregoing is an attempt to reconstruct the literary companionship Fitzgerald enjoyed with Edmund Wilson. Wilson, himself a novelist, playwright, and versatile critic with far-ranging interests, was, as the particulars indicate, Scott Fitzgerald's friend and adviser from the beginning of the novelist's career to its end. "For twenty years," Fitzgerald wrote in 1936, "a certain man had been my intellectual conscience. That was Edmund Wilson." What this history suggests is that Fitzgerald, if not altogether happy in the association, was at least fortunate in the effect it had on his understanding and his work. He might have derived more gratification, in a superficial sense, from someone who was quicker to accept and to praise. But from the beginning Fitzgerald had profound respect for Wilson's opinion, and ultimately he came to value the discipline and the striving for perfection that Wilson demanded. "The thing that lies behind all great careers," he confided to his daughter not long before he died, "is the sense that life is essentially a cheat and its conditions are those of defeat, and that the redeeming things are not 'happiness and pleasure,' but the deeper satisfactions that come out of struggle."

Throughout, Wilson's influence was general rather than particular, indirect rather than immediate. He remained unobtrusively in the background, something of a symbol in Fitzgerald's imagination, representative of artistic integrity and intellectual mastery of the materials of life. Even so, Wilson did more to shape Fitzgerald's career than any of the other writers with whom the novelist enjoyed close association.

An index to Fitzgerald's indebtedness to Wilson may be seen in a summary of his progress as a novelist, which in large measure was guided by Wilson's suggestion. After the publication of *This Side of Paradise* Wilson correctly assumed that Fitzgerald had taken his hero too seriously. "Cultivate a universal irony," Wilson advised. Two years later Fitzgerald brought out *The Beautiful and Damned,* which begins: "Irony was the final polish of the shoe, the ultimate dab of the clothes brush, a sort of intellectual 'There!'" The book concludes: "That exquisite heavenly irony which has tabulated the demise of many generations of sparrows. . . ." Wilson also recommended that Fitzgerald broaden his limited acquaintance with the work of other writers: "Do read something other than contemporary British novelists." *The Beautiful and Damned* and *The Great Gatsby* demonstrate that Fitzgerald heeded Wilson's counsel.

Although Wilson thought Fitzgerald's second novel an improvement over *This Side of Paradise,* he still found cause for dissatisfaction with his friend's work up to that point. "His restless imagination may yet produce something durable," Wilson wrote in his article for *The Bookman* in 1922. "For the present, however, this imagination is certainly not seen to the best advantage: it suffers badly from lack of discipline and poverty of aesthetic ideas. Fitzgerald is a dazzling extemporizer, but his stories have a way of petering out: he seems never to have planned them completely or to have thought out his themes from the beginning."

The Great Gatsby, written two years later, reveals a rich awareness of what Wilson called "aesthetic ideas," by which he meant, as I understand it, the controlling principles which dictate the artistic treatment of material. And the discipline of Fitzgerald's imagination in *The Great Gatsby* is apparent: a later critic has called *Gatsby* "the most perfect example of a planned novel in our modern tradition—planned in [the] mathematical sense of a Bach concerto." [6] It is as if Fitzgerald had taken to heart each of Wilson's strictures in 1922 and had labored to satisfy his friend's most rigid requirements for achievement in the art of the novel.

The Great Gatsby was probably the finest product of Wilson's influence on Fitzgerald. As we have seen, *Tender Is the Night* was written during a period when the strong personal attachment between the two men had suffered some attenuation. But the fact that Wilson offered repeated encouragement to Fitzgerald during the composition of *The Last Tycoon* indicates that the relationship continued, if somewhat diminished in its force, up to the time of Fitzgerald's death. And Wilson's crucial services to Fitzgerald's posthumous recognition suggest the extent of the critic's devoted interest. The judgment of the nineteen-fifties and early sixties confirms Wilson's endorsements. More than that: it marks the triumph of Wilson's personal endeavors on behalf of his friend.

In 1922, Edmund Wilson remarked that Scott Fitzgerald had not learned to adapt his talents to their best uses: Fitzgerald was a young man, Wilson wrote, who "had been left with a rare jewel which he doesn't know quite what to do with." Twenty years later in his dedicatory verses for *The Crack-Up*, Wilson returned to the jewel image as a metaphorical means of evaluating Fitzgerald's fiction: he envisioned his friend's literary works as "jewels, in a handful, lying loose." The short stories were seen as

> Flawed amethysts; the moonstone's milky blues;
> Chill blues of pale transparent tourmaline;
> Opals of shifty yellow, chartreuse green,

[6] Maxwell Geismar, *The Last of the Provincials* (New York, 1959), p. 315.

Wherein a vein vermilion flees and flickers—
Tight phials of the spirit's light mixed liquors;
Some tinsel zircons, common turquoise. . . .

And Fitzgerald's most perfectly realized works—*The Great Gatsby* and *The Last Tycoon*—were given special prominence by the appraiser of literary gems:

Two emeralds, green and lucid, one half-cut,
One cut consummately—both take their place
In Letters' most expensive Cartier case.

The concluding lines of Wilson's poem suggest the depth of his personal loss:

[I] dread to know
Those eyes struck dark, dissolving in a wrecked
And darkened world, that gleam of intellect
That spilled into the spectrum of tune, taste,
Scent, color, living speech, is gone, is lost.

Thus Wilson, friend and critic, recapitulates in his brief elegy the two aspects of his relationship which, taken together, form its essence.

Fitzgerald's attitude is revealed in a letter to Wilson written in 1939, as he was about to enter the last year of his life:

Believe me, Bunny, it meant more to me than it could possibly have meant to you to see you that evening. It seemed to renew old times learning about Franz Kafka and latter things that are going on in the world of poetry, because I am still the ignoramus that you and John Bishop wrote about at Princeton.

With these words Fitzgerald sounded the keynote which prevailed, for him, from beginning to end. There is ample evidence to show that his humility was rewarded—in the enduring excellence of his art.

CHAPTER III

H. L. Mencken

> "Sophisticated—God, I'm sophisticated."
> —DAISY BUCHANAN

Fitzgerald's dream of success had suffered a serious setback in the spring of 1919. We have already seen how many difficulties beset the young Midwesterner who, after his discharge from the Army, had earnestly aspired to become a cosmopolitan man of letters; and we have seen the failure of that ambitious undertaking. Toward the end of his stay in the city, Zelda Sayre had made known her decision to let Fitzgerald go his own way—which was, after a few weeks of hesitation, back to St. Paul, where he retired to ruminate on "debts, despair, and a broken engagement. . . ."

But apparently Fitzgerald's frustrations served only to increase his determination. He worked harder than ever at revising his novel; by September it was finished and on its way to Maxwell Perkins at Scribner's. The immediate sequel is well known. With acceptance, Fitzgerald's world changed; the youthful author who a few months earlier had tasted the sobering drafts of defeat now found himself intoxicated on the wine of his achievement.

If it is true that "too early success spoiled him," as one of Fitzgerald's friends remarked later—made him unfit to cope with the reverses of maturer years—the emotions of his moment of fulfillment, in any case, obliterated all the anguish of previous disappointments. For Fitzgerald, the acceptance of *This Side of Paradise* meant new assurance and self-regard; it meant Zelda Sayre; it meant a return, several months later, to New York City. By that time the transition from amateur to professional had been accomplished. Before *This Side of Paradise* appeared, Fitzgerald had sold fifteen stories to a number of popular magazines; he had begun a new novel; and he had "discovered" H. L. Mencken, who was to leave a strong impression on the fiction Fitzgerald produced during the next two years.

In an interview with Thomas Boyd in the summer of 1921, Fitzgerald revealed that "it was not until after I got the proofs of my book back from the publishers that I learned of Mencken. I happened across The Smart Set one day and I thought 'Here's a man whose name I ought to know. I guess I'll stick it in the proof sheets.'"[1]

The periodical Fitzgerald refers to, a copy of which he "happened across" in the late fall of 1919, had by that time become one of the most influential and widely read *avant-garde* publications of the period. H. L. Mencken and George Jean Nathan had become coeditors of the magazine in 1914; thereafter *The Smart Set* (which had previously been dedi-

---

[1] The passage Fitzgerald inserted in *This Side of Paradise:* "[Amory Blaine] read enormously. He was puzzled and depressed by 'A Portrait of the Artist as a Young Man'; intensely interested by 'Joan and Peter' and 'The Undying Fire,' and rather surprised by his discovery through a critic named Mencken of several excellent novels: 'Vandover and the Brute,' 'The Damnation of Theron Ware,' and 'Jennie Gerhardt.'"

cated to romantic and near-pornographic fiction) became a source of amusing and sophisticated commentary for thousands of American readers during the decade it was in operation under its two famous editors.

Part of its appeal, of course, was the fresh irreverence that filled its pages, the knowledgeable reviews of current books and plays, Mencken's unorthodoxy and Nathan's worldliness, the implicit understanding that *The Smart Set* was for "civilized" readers. But aside from its urbanity, the magazine also provided a wealth of vivid material by new and unknown writers. Manuscripts that had been rejected by other Eastern periodicals were assured careful consideration at *The Smart Set* offices, and the hospitality of its editors gave a great many discouraged young writers their first bit of deserved recognition. Some of these unknowns later achieved wider renown, so that a list of early contributors to *The Smart Set* reads like a roster of twentieth-century literary luminaries. James Branch Cabell published a sketch in the magazine which he called "Some Ladies and Jurgen"; the sketch was later developed into the famous novel. James Joyce appeared in *The Smart Set* with stories of Dublin life, at a time when he was virtually unknown to American readers. Eugene O'Neill, one of Nathan's discoveries, was brought out in *The Smart Set*. Somerset Maugham's "Miss Thompson," later dramatized as *Rain*, was published in *The Smart Set* after it had been rejected by a dozen New York editors. Theodore Dreiser, Sherwood Anderson, and D. H. Lawrence were among the contributors of new and original fiction. James Huneker, Waldo Frank, and Thomas Beer published critical commentary in its pages. Fitzgerald himself, as already noted, made his first professional appearance in this lively and important journal.[2]

[2] See William Manchester, *Disturber of the Peace* (New York, 1951), pp. 78-80.

Fitzgerald had met Mencken in the summer of 1920; he had read *The Smart Set;* he was profoundly impressed. In a review of Mencken's *Prejudices: Second Series,* Fitzgerald claimed that Mencken had done "more for the national letters than any man alive." And in a speech delivered to the Women's City Club in St. Paul in 1921, Fitzgerald hailed Mencken as "a man who has, I believe, done more for contemporary American literature than any other man alive."

Fitzgerald's admiration for Mencken might be defended on objective grounds; notwithstanding the tone of youthful extravagance, a great deal of evidence supports the younger man's nomination of Mencken to a position of supreme importance. Before Mencken's advent upon the American literary scene, before his championship of Dreiser and Cabell and his impatience with the spurious and timid fictionists who dominated the popular market during the early decades of the century, there had been no voice clear or strong enough to stir native intellectuals to articulate protest, or to define the specific cultural deficiencies of the time. Mencken's resistance to censorship, too, and his readiness to encourage the unorthodox and the original played a significant part in the growing vitality and forthright realism that was to characterize the fiction of the nineteen-twenties. If it is true that Mencken was not always reliable as an arbiter of literary taste, if he cherished his sometimes outrageous opinions to the point of dogmatism and suffered from notorious critical blind spots, it is equally true that he inspired into fulfillment a great deal of the vigor that was latent in our literature. Even Alfred Kazin, whose portrait of Mencken in *On Native Grounds* is dominantly unsympathetic, concedes that Mencken rallied all the new young writers together and gave to his era the gift of high humor. "If Mencken had never lived," writes Kazin, "it would have taken a whole army of assorted philosophers, monologists,

editors, and patrons of the new writing to make up for him."
We might question Fitzgerald's authority for issuing *ex
cathedra* pronouncements on Mencken's place in "the national letters," but there is no doubt a great deal of truth in
his appraisal of the man who exerted such a powerful influence on an entire literary generation.

Fitzgerald's enthusiasm was also prompted by tempera-
ment, by the instinct which guided him to the company of
writers whose influence might prove valuable. The young
Fitzgerald was susceptible to new forces, both professional
and personal, which promised development and increased
maturity. H. L. Mencken, along with George Jean Nathan,
represented both of these—and something more. To the
newly arrived author from the Midwest, still unaccustomed
to the wider world of the New York literati, the editors of
The Smart Set must have seemed the ultimate in sophistication, a quality which the young novelist began assiduously
to cultivate.

Mencken's reaction to Fitzgerald was encouraging. The
former had been favorably impressed by *This Side of Paradise;* and the stories Fitzgerald submitted to *The Smart Set*
were promptly accepted. Eight of Fitzgerald's stories
appeared in the magazine in 1921 and 1922; among them
were "May Day" and "The Diamond as Big as the Ritz"—
certainly among the very best of Fitzgerald's fiction during
this period. No doubt Fitzgerald was flattered by this reception, coming as it did from the most famous editor of the
era. At the same time Fitzgerald's attitude reflects his
profound respect for Mencken's critical judgment: "I'd
rather have you like a book of mine," he wrote Mencken,
"than anyone else in America."

Yet Fitzgerald was never to achieve with Mencken the
close friendship he enjoyed with Edmund Wilson or, for a
time, with Ring Lardner. Mencken was a confirmed hater

of New York; he spent only a small part of his time in the city, attending chiefly to his own editorial affairs. After his business was concluded he returned to Baltimore. Thus, although the older man visited Fitzgerald at the latter's home in Great Neck (1923-1924), and although the two writers carried on an extensive correspondence, their meetings were infrequent. Furthermore, Mencken's attitude toward friendship was completely unsentimental: "A prudent man," he once wrote, "remembering that life is short, gives an hour or two, now and then, to a critical examination of his friendships. He weighs them, edits them, tests the metal of them. A few he retains, perhaps with radical changes in their terms. But the majority he expunges from his minutes and tries to forget, as he tries to forget the cold and clammy loves of year before last." As we shall see presently, Mencken was sometimes governed by such "prudence" in his relations with Scott Fitzgerald.

It is clear, however, that Mencken considered Fitzgerald one of the most promising and brilliant members of the younger generation of writers just coming into power at the beginning of the decade. But this opinion (which he documented in a review of *The Great Gatsby* in 1925) was not without critical reservations. In Fitzgerald's first two novels, Mencken remarked, the writing was "slipshod—at times almost illiterate." Fitzgerald could treat character and situation with great skill, but he had no great talent with words. *The Great Gatsby*, however, was a different matter: "There are pages so artfully contrived that one can no more imagine improvising them than one can imagine improvising a fugue. They are full of little delicacies, charming turns of phrase, penetrating second thoughts." Nevertheless, Mencken insisted, somewhat perversely, *This Side of Paradise* was vastly superior. He thought *Gatsby* "no more than a glorified anecdote." The character and the plot of the novel, Mencken said, were obviously unimportant; *Gatsby* was not to be put on the same shelf with *This Side of Paradise.*

Several months later Fitzgerald published an essay, "How to Waste Material: A Note on my Generation," parts of which indicate a subtle modification of his earlier enthusiasm for Mencken. Most of the writers who had shown such promise in the early twenties, Fitzgerald wrote in his essay, had sadly disappointed all expectations of their producing a golden age; and to a limited extent this was the fault of H. L. Mencken.

> What Mencken felt the absence of, what he wanted, and justly, back in 1920, got away from him, got twisted in his hand. Not because the "literary revolution" went beyond him but because his idea had always been ethical rather than aesthetic. In the history of culture no pure aesthetic idea has ever served as an offensive weapon. Mencken's invective, sharp as Swift's, made its point by the use of the most forceful prose style now written in English. Immediately, instead of committing himself to an infinite series of pronouncements upon the American novel, he should have modulated his tone to the more urbane, more critical one of his early essay on Dreiser.
>
> But perhaps it was already too late. Already he had begotten a family of hammer and tongs men—insensitive, suspicious of glamour, preoccupied exclusively with the external, the contemptible, the "national" and the drab, whose style was a debasement of his least effective manner and who, like glib children, played continually with his themes in his maternal shadow.

Elsewhere in the essay Fitzgerald invokes the old refrain of the early twenties: "Mencken has done more for American letters than any man alive." Yet now, four or five years later, what Mencken has done has not been entirely beneficial. Fitzgerald's objections are rather fuzzily presented: on the one hand, Mencken's critical interests were ethical rather than aesthetic; on the other, Mencken's imitators have been too numerous and uninspired. But the reasons for Fitzgerald's dissatisfaction are perhaps clarified if we assume some element of personal resentment against Mencken's criticism of *Gatsby*. Soon after he had read Mencken's review, Fitzgerald wrote Edmund Wilson: "Without making any invidious comparisons between Class A and Class C, if my novel is an anecdote so is *The Brothers Karamazoff*. From one angle the latter could be reduced into a detective story." [3] Fitzgerald might well have been annoyed at the fact that Mencken, while approving the style of *The Great Gatsby* (that is, its "aesthetic" excellence), did not think the novel important as a criticism of American life (that is, its "ethical" value). I have spoken earlier of Mencken's occasional "blind spots," of which his review of *Gatsby* might serve as an example. Fitzgerald's novel is as cogent a comment on American life as was made during the decade.

Whatever the causes for the decline of Fitzgerald's admiration for Mencken, it is certain that their personal relations suffered moments of severe strain. Mencken's cold-blooded attitude toward some of his friends could take the form of brutal tactlessness, as one painful anecdote, recounted by Charles Angoff in his book on Mencken, illustrates. Sometime in the late twenties Mencken and Angoff paid Fitzgerald a visit in his New York hotel suite.

"I have an idea for a novel going through my head," Fitzgerald told Mencken. "Have a lot of it written up. It's about a woman who wants to destroy a man because she

[3] But to Mencken Fitzgerald wrote respectfully that his review was "just and illuminating," and that he, Fitzgerald, was deeply grateful for Mencken's continued interest and enthusiasm.

loves him too much and is afraid she'll lose him, but not to another woman—but because she'll stop loving him so much. Well, she decides to destroy him by marrying him. She marries him, and gets to love him even more than she did before. Then she gets jealous of him, because of his achievements in some line that she thinks she's also good in. Then, I guess, she commits suicide—first she does it step by step, the way all people, all women commit suicide, by drinking, by sleeping around, by being impolite to friends, and that way. I haven't got the rest of it clear in my head, but that's the heart of it. What do you think, Henry?"

"Well, it's your wife, Zelda, all over again," Mencken said.

Fitzgerald sat down, swallowed some of his drink, and then got up and paced back and forth. Without looking at Mencken, he said: "That's the dumbest piece of literary criticism I have ever heard or read."

Mencken said nothing. Fitzgerald continued: "You know, Henry, sometimes I think you're no literary critic at all. I don't know what the hell you are, but you're no critic, that's sure. I spill my insides to you and you answer with . . . Zelda. You don't know what a writer goes through, what he fumbles for, you don't know the grace he searches for. And, goddamn it, you have no compassion. Of all the times to mention Zelda to me! Of all the goddamn times to mention her!" He sank into his chair and burst into tears.

Mencken stood up, muttered, "I'll be seeing you," and he and I walked out.

"Scott will never amount to a hoot in hell till he gets rid of his wife," Mencken said as we returned to the office.[4]

The incident fits the mood of the late twenties, the period, as Fitzgerald wrote later, of "wide-spread neurosis" which heralded the personal and national catastrophes to come. Mencken and Fitzgerald saw little of each other during these years.

[4] *H. L. Mencken: A Portrait from Memory* (New York, 1956), pp. 98-99.

In the early thirties, after Fitzgerald had taken up residence at Rodgers Forge, just outside Baltimore, the two men resumed for a while the congenial evenings they had enjoyed in the early days of their friendship. But this phase of the relationship was short-lived. Fitzgerald was drinking heavily, and Zelda was suffering from an increased tendency toward psychosis; she was, in fact, dividing her time between uneasy visits at home under Fitzgerald's supervision, and long confinements in a mental institution. The strain and tension in the Fitzgerald home were strongly evident. Mencken, meanwhile, had been married in 1930 to Sara Haardt, a literary lady from Montgomery, Alabama—the same town where Zelda Sayre had spent her younger years as a well-known belle. It was natural that Sara Mencken should take an interest in the Fitzgeralds, and that she should pay them repeated visits: Sara had known Zelda when they were both residents of Montgomery. But Mencken, who had a strong distaste for the kind of disorder that now threatened to engulf Fitzgerald and his wife, soon told Sara to discontinue all social calls at the house in Rodgers Forge.

At this time Fitzgerald, unaware of Mencken's attitude, was preparing *The Great Gatsby* for publication in The Modern Library series. In his introduction he harked back to the theme of Mencken's contribution to American literature; the tone of his comments—marked by nostalgic sentiment and admiration—was no doubt quickened by the two writers' recent renewal of friendly relations:

> I think the writers of my time were spoiled [Fitzgerald wrote], living in generous days when there was plenty of space on the page for endless ratiocination about fiction—a space largely created by Mencken because of his disgust for what passed as criticism before he arrived and made his public. They were encouraged by his bravery and his

tremendous and profound love of letters. . . . I don't think many men of my age can regard him without reverence. . . . To any new effort by a new man he brought an attitude; he made many mistakes . . . but he came equipped; he never had to go back for his tools.

And now that he has abandoned American fiction to its own devices, there is no one to take his place. [The writers of the early twenties were accorded] an appreciation of the world of imagination in which they had been trying, with greater or lesser success, to live—the world that Mencken made stable in the days when he was watching over us.

This was Fitzgerald's final tribute to H. L. Mencken. By the time it was written, both writers had undergone a decline in popularity; the era in which they had reigned, each in his own way, was dead. Yet during those early years Fitzgerald had emerged from provincial America to become one of our most mature and sophisticated craftsmen—which is to say that his second novel, written while he was under Mencken's influence, was a step forward in his development toward the controlled excellence of later works. But it is to *The Beautiful and Damned* that we must now turn if we wish to understand this important stage in Fitzgerald's development.

II

Fitzgerald's novel *The Beautiful and Damned* and his play *The Vegetable* were both produced during the early nineteen-twenties, the period when his association with H. L. Mencken was at its height. A comparison of these works with the essays Mencken published around the same time suggests quite clearly the extent of Fitzgerald's debt to the famous polemicist of the postwar decade. In the first place, Fitzgerald's treatment of character in *The Beautiful and Damned* owes much to Mencken's comments in "The

National Letters," a long essay published in the volume *Prejudices: Second Series*—a book, it will be remembered, which Fitzgerald reviewed early in 1921. Mencken claims in his essay that American literature exhibits "not a man of delicate organization in revolt against the inexplicable tragedy of existence, but a man of low sensibilities and elemental desires yielding himself gladly to his environment, and so achieving what, under a third-rate civilization, passes for success." Civilized readers, Mencken goes on to say, find it impossible to take an interest in these inferior (i.e., typically American) works of the bourgeois imagination. On the contrary, sophisticated men want to read about the conflict between the individual and "the harsh, meaningless fiats of destiny, the unintelligible mandates and vagaries of God." The true fictional hero is not one who yields and wins, but one who resists and fails. "Character in decay," Mencken concludes with somewhat arbitrary logic, "is thus the theme of the great bulk of superior fiction." These dicta, as James E. Miller has observed in his study of Fitzgerald's works, are sharply reflected in the hero and heroine in *The Beautiful and Damned*.[5]

More specific points of influence, in addition to general conception of character, are to be found throughout Fitzgerald's novel. We might compare, for example, Fitzgerald's comments on America's entry into World War I, as they appear in *The Beautiful and Damned*, with equivalent passages in *This Side of Paradise*. Amory Blaine's reaction, in the earlier novel, reflects the popular American sentiment toward involvement in the European crisis: "He knew he was going to have a bad week. Not that he doubted the war—Germany stood for everything repugnant to him; for materialism and the direction of tremendous licentious

[5] Miller, *The Fictional Technique of Scott Fitzgerald* (The Hague, 1957), pp. 39-41.

force." *The Beautiful and Damned* sounds a somewhat different note:

> In April war was declared with Germany. Wilson and his cabinet—a cabinet that in its lack of distinction was strangely reminiscent of the twelve apostles—let loose the carefully starved dogs of war, and the press began to whoop hysterically against the sinister morals, sinister philosophy, and sinister music produced by the Teutonic temperament. Those who fancied themselves particularly broad-minded made the exquisite distinction that it was only the German Government which aroused them to hysteria; the rest were worked up to a condition of retching indecency. Any song which contained the word "mother" and the word "kaiser" was assured of tremendous success. At last everyone had something to talk about—and almost everyone fully enjoyed it, as though they had been cast for parts in a sombre and romantic play.

Surely the difference here is the product of Fitzgerald's exposure to H. L. Mencken. Amory Blaine may safely entertain hostility against the Germans; but Anthony Patch (the hero of *The Beautiful and Damned*) dare not evoke such sentiments for fear of including himself among the super-patriots against whom Mencken fulminated. Anti-anti-German sentiment was, in fact, one of the latter's favorite themes during the early twenties; and one of its fiercest expressions is found in the essay "Star Spangled Men," in which Mencken excoriates editorial writers of Eastern newspapers who stressed anti-German propaganda in their columns, agitators who denounced all German music, and other elements of the American public who contributed to the general hysteria. "Star Spangled Men" appeared in *The New Republic* for September, 1920—an issue Fitzgerald almost certainly read while he was writing *The Beautiful and Damned*.

Another instance of Mencken's influence on *The Beautiful and Damned* is reflected in Fitzgerald's treatment of democratic government. Fitzgerald had touched upon this theme earlier, in *This Side of Paradise,* when Amory Blaine speculates on the possibility of educating the common man, purging him of "platitudes and prejudices and sentimentalisms." If such education cannot be accomplished, muses Fitzgerald's hero, then it doesn't matter what happens "to man or his systems." Such political theorizing, obviously, has little force or direction.

But similar commentary in *The Beautiful and Damned* is much more pointed; Fitzgerald sounds the tone of condescension so reminiscent of Mencken, the scorn and the ire—half amused, half indignant, as when Anthony Patch indulges in a peculiar daydream:

> He tried to imagine himself in Congress rooting around in that incredible pigsty with the narrow and porcine brows he saw pictured sometimes in the rotogravure sections of the Sunday newspapers, those glorified proletarians babbling blandly to the nation the ideas of high-school seniors. Little men with copy-book ambitions who by mediocrity had thought to emerge from mediocrity into the lustreless and unromantic heaven of a government by the people—and the best, the dozen shrewd men at the top, egotistic and cynical, were content to lead this choir of white ties and wire collar-buttons in a discordant and amazing hymn, compounded of a vague confusion between wealth as a reward for virtue and wealth as a proof of vice, and continued cheers for God, the Constitution, and the Rocky Mountains!

And one of Mencken's favorite devices—the outrageous afterthought—appears in Maury Noble's comment: "I'm all for criminals—give color to life. Trouble is if you started to punish ignorance you'd have to begin in the first families, then you could take up the moving picture people, and finally Congress and the clergy."

These passages, which so clearly reflect Fitzgerald's borrowed attitudes, anticipate the theme and tone of *The Vegetable*, the political farce-comedy Fitzgerald wrote immediately after *The Beautiful and Damned*. We might interrupt our discussion of the novel at this point and, since most of the content of Fitzgerald's play was inspired by Mencken's comments on democratic government, submit *The Vegetable* to a brief examination. First, it is not unlikely that Fitzgerald got the title itself from his reading in H. L. Mencken. In his essay "On Being an American," first published around the time Fitzgerald was writing his play, Mencken writes: "Here is a country in which all political thought and activity are concentrated upon the scramble for jobs—in which the normal politician, whether he be President or a village road supervisor, is willing to renounce any principle, however precious to him, and to adopt any lunacy, however offensive to him, in order to keep his place at the trough. . . . here is a country in which it is an axiom that a businessman shall be a member of the Chamber of Commerce, an admirer of Charles M. Schwab, a reader of the *Saturday Evening Post*, a golfer—in brief, a vegetable." It might not be coincidental, too, that Fitzgerald's hero in the play makes his entrance yelling for his copy of the *Saturday Evening Post*.

The Vegetable is the story of Jerry Frost, a fifty-dollar-a-week clerk in a railroad office, who confesses to a visiting efficiency expert that he has lost all ambition, but that in his youth he wanted to be a postman. Later on in the first act, Jerry admits to his nagging wife that he has at times cherished a dream of becoming President. When she laughs at this, Jerry accuses her of having killed his ambition.

The central episode in the play occurs in Act II, which dramatizes Jerry's dream fantasy. He has been elected President and is surrounded by friends and relatives who have been introduced in Act I. "Dada," Jerry's blind, deaf, and senile father, has become Secretary of the Treasury. Joseph Fish, who is the fiancé of Jerry's sister-in-law, emerges in the fantasy as the Senator from Idaho (in the first act Fish has confided to Jerry his ambition to be a Senator: "That's where you get the *real* graft"). And Mr. Snooks, Jerry's bootlegger, is transformed into the Ambassador from Irish-Poland.

Fitzgerald introduces several complications in Act II: "Dada," it is revealed, has "emptied" the Treasury—he can't recall whether he buried the money or dumped it in the ocean; Jerry buys the Buzzard Islands from Ambassador Snooks; General Pushing invents reasons to declare war on Irish-Poland; and Jerry is impeached while a jazz band plays Suwanee River. Just before the hero is sentenced by Judge Fossile, Jerry declares that he doesn't want to be President after all. "Just try electing me again," he threatens. "We won't," answers the General. "As a President you'd make a good postman." At this point, presumably, Jerry awakens from his dream, and the curtain descends on Act II.

Act III discovers a new and different Jerry Frost—a happy husband who has recaptured the admiration of his wife and a man who has found his métier as a benevolent and highly efficient postman. Thus ends *The Vegetable*, Fitzgerald's one endeavor at full-length drama and his most notable artistic misfortune.

The dramatic complications at the center of the play—scattered arbitrarily and almost haphazardly through Act II—demonstrate Fitzgerald's interest in a number of topical themes celebrated by Mencken. There is once again the satire on anti-German sentiment already noted in *The Beautiful and Damned*. General Pushing, after announcing the news that the United States has declared war on Irish-Poland, informs President Jerry that the Army is planning to capture the Buzzard Islands:

> We've ordered all stuffed Buzzards to be removed from the natural history museums. (Cheers.) And domestic Buzzards are now fair game, both in and out of season. (More cheers.) Buzzard domination would be unthinkable.

And there is the newsboy who delivers Jerry's newspaper, and pointing to a dinner jacket Jerry is wearing, proudly announces: "I almost had a dress suit myself once. I hadda get one so I could take a high degree in the Ku Klux Klan." Mencken's references to the Ku Klux Klan (all contemptuous) are frequent during this period; two specific instances occur in the essays "Star Spangled Men" and "On Being an American."

Aside from these minor episodes it seems clear that Fitzgerald's principal themes in the play were inspired by Mencken: *The Vegetable* comments generally and implicitly on government by corruption, government by stupidity, and government by absurdity. "I hold that this elevation of politics to the place of undiluted comedy is peculiarly American," wrote Mencken in an essay published the same year *The Vegetable* was staged—"that nowhere else on this disreputable ball has the art of the sham-battle been developed to such fineness. . . . Here politics is purged of all menace, all sinister quality, all genuine significance, and stuffed with such gorgeous humors, such inordinate farce that one comes to the end of a campaign with one's ribs loose. . . ." Small wonder that a reviewer of *The Vegetable* (John F. Carter in the New York *Post*) commented: "The spirit of the play is an obvious act of deference to Mencken's virulent contempt for the American people." [6]

Yet there is no virulence in Fitzgerald's drama, and precious little contempt—at least of the kind that makes Mencken's commentary pungent reading today. What is obviously lacking in *The Vegetable* is the development of any one of the several themes—or the sense of understanding that animates the comic episodes in some of Fitzgerald's better works. Compare *The Vegetable* with the comic fantasy "The Diamond as Big as the Ritz," where the novelist's irony is firmly grounded in familiar and cogent personal experience, and Fitzgerald's relative ignorance in the play is clearly demonstrated. In writing *The Vegetable* Fitzgerald was following a false lead: the materials and tone of the play were not his own.

Still, the influence of Mencken here is not altogether without value and significance in the young novelist's development. Fitzgerald's treatment of the themes of ambition, the American dream, and political chicanery is superficial; but his *awareness* of these themes as material for fiction represents a step forward in his growing sophistication and his understanding of national experience. Other themes and subjects exploited by Mencken, which are related to those I have noted in *The Vegetable*, appear in *The Beautiful and Damned*—in which Fitzgerald presented his material in greater depth, though by no means with perfect artistic detachment.

Mencken's influence on Fitzgerald's second novel is most evident in the character of the hero, Anthony Patch, and in the passages devoted to speculation on America's social structure. There are other important themes, of course—more personal ones, which it will be advisable to consider

[6] Quoted by Arthur Mizener in *The Far Side of Paradise* (Cambridge, 1951), p. 156.

first before moving on to the Menckenian episodes. Into *The Beautiful and Damned* Fitzgerald projected his most poignant feelings of delight and disappointment as a husband in the early years of his marriage to Zelda Sayre; he dramatized his fear of becoming a second-rate literary hack; and he delineated what Paul Rosenfeld called "the external clatter, movement and boldness of privileged post-adolescent America."

The first of these motifs appears in Anthony's growing understanding of his relationship with his wife Gloria—a relationship that undergoes emotional developments ranging from sentimental sweetness to violent conflict, and finally to resignation and indifference.

The second motif—perhaps the most personal that appears in the novel—is evident in Fitzgerald's depiction of Richard Caramel, the author who produces a sensational best-seller called "The Demon Lover" (the title of one of Fitzgerald's own projected, but never completed, novels). Midway through *The Beautiful and Damned* Caramel confesses to Anthony Patch: "I'm certainly writing faster and I don't seem to be thinking as much as I used to. Perhaps it's because I don't get any conversation, now that you're married and Maury's gone to Philadelphia. Haven't the old urge and ambition. Early success and all that." Near the end of the novel we discover that Caramel has indeed succumbed to his own success, that it has blinded his faculty for self-criticism and spoiled him with its easy rewards: Caramel has become a byword among the critics for commercialism and trashiness. Fitzgerald's apprehension over the possible decay of his own talent is reflected in his portrayal of Richard Caramel.

The third motif consists of the actions and manners of the young protagonists and their comrades—the detailed surface representation of the parties they attend, the turns of their conversation, the expressive gestures of their clothes and cars and apartments and homes, their cozy winter afternoons at the Plaza, the key and pitch and tempo of their conduct—all of which are rendered, as in the passage below, in Fitzgerald's characteristic early manner:

> As they entered, the orchestra were sounding the preliminary whimpers of a maxixe, a tune full of castanets and facile faintly languorous violin harmonies, appropriate to the crowded winter grill teeming with an excited college crowd, high-spirited at the approach of the holidays. Carefully, Gloria considered several locations, and rather to Anthony's annoyance paraded him circuitously to a table for two at the far side of the room. Reaching it she again considered. Would she sit on the right or the left? Her beautiful eyes and lips were very grave as she made her choice, and Anthony thought again how naive was her every gesture; she took all the things of life for hers to choose and apportion, as though she were continually picking out presents for herself from an inexhaustible counter.

Underlying these motifs in *The Beautiful and Damned* is an interest in American class structure—a substratum of meaning that takes the form of an inconclusive quest for some clarification of our notions about wealth, aristocracy, and social aspiration. Some of Fitzgerald's early stories, "The Diamond as Big as the Ritz," for example, and "The Offshore Pirate," show that the novelist had been attracted to these themes for some time. But it is Mencken who gave Fitzgerald's thoughts on these subjects some definite shape and direction.

The Beautiful and Damned is essentially a fable of the parvenu in reverse. The novel concentrates on one figure Anthony Patch, and traces his decline from the leisure class through various strata of the middle class until he arrives, near the conclusion, at a condition of financial and social bankruptcy. At the first extreme we encounter Anthony Patch the young man about town with an inherited income and a steady faith in his own uselessness, which he assumes is part of the privilege of his position: "I do nothing," Anthony admits casually. "I do nothing, for there's nothing I can do that's worth doing." Aimlessly, the hero lays plans to write a history of the Middle Ages—a project which he dreams about from time to time, but which he never begins. Thus portrayed, Anthony Patch qualifies in a number of ways as a member of Mencken's *intelligentsia*, a class Mencken defined in his essay "The National Letters." The American *intelligentsia*, Mencken wrote, displays "all the marks of a caste of learned and sagacious men—a great book knowledge . . . not a few gestures that suggest the aristocrat. But under the surface one quickly discovers that the whole thing is little more than play-acting, and not always very skillful." In the same essay Mencken speaks of the distinctive qualities of American thought as follows: "American thinking, when it concerns itself with beautiful letters as when it concerns itself with religious dogma or political theory, is extraordinarily timid and superficial . . . the outward virtues it undoubtedly shows are always the virtues, not of profundity, not of courage, not of originality, but merely those of an emasculated and often very trashy dilettantism." Fitzgerald's hero is a more complicated character than Mencken's exaggerated American "thinker"; yet Anthony's attempts at intellectual attainment follow the pattern Mencken traces in "The National Letters."

In the background of *The Beautiful and Damned* Fitzgerald has placed the dim figure of Adam Patch, Anthony's grandfather. Adam is the force that controls Anthony's destiny, the promise of thirty million dollars which would justify the younger man's elegant hollowness and support his determination to do nothing. Grandfather Patch lives

an isolated existence in Tarrytown, to which he has retired
in middle age after having amassed a fortune in Wall Street.
From his country estate Adam devotes his thoughts and
energies to "the moral regeneration of the world":

> He became a reformer among reformers. Emulating the
> magnificent efforts of Anthony Comstock, after whom his
> grandson was named, he levelled a varied assortment of
> uppercuts and body-blows at liquor, literature, vice, art,
> patent medicines, and Sunday theatres. His mind, under
> the influence of that insidious mildew which eventually
> forms on all but the few, gave itself up furiously to every
> indignation of the age. From an armchair in the office of
> his Tarrytown estate he directed against the enormous
> hypothetical enemy, unrighteousness, a campaign which
> went on through fifteen years, during which he displayed
> himself a rabid monomaniac, an unqualified nuisance and
> an intolerable bore.

Perhaps, as James E. Miller suggests, Adam Patch is Fitzgerald's personification of a dying Victorianism. Yet he is
something else as well. Mencken devotes considerable space
in "The National Letters" to a cynical examination of the
class represented by Anthony's grandfather:

> I need not set out at any length, I hope, the intellectual
> deficiencies of the plutocracy—its utter failure to show any-
> thing even remotely resembling the making of an aristoc-
> racy. It is badly educated, it is stupid, it is full of low-caste
> superstitions and indignations, it is without decent traditions
> or informing vision; above all, it is extraordinarily lacking
> in the most elemental independence and courage. Out of
> this class come the grotesque fashionable society of our big
> towns, already described. Imagine a horde of peasants in-
> credibly enriched and with almost infinite power thrust into
> their hands, and you will have a fair picture of its habitual

state of mind. It shows all the stigmata of inferiority—moral
certainty, cruelty, suspicion of ideas, fear. . . . Obviously
there is no aristocracy here. One finds only one of the
necessary elements, and that only in the plutocracy, to wit,
a truculent egoism.

In addition, Fitzgerald's familiar references to Anthony
Comstock are in all probability derived from Mencken, who
sprinkled his pages liberally with allusions to "the Emperor
of Wowsers."

Whether or not Fitzgerald accepted Mencken's ideas on
the American plutocracy is hard to say; but it seems certain
that in the character of Adam Patch the novelist meant to
portray the Menckenian plutocracy created by equalitarian
government. Anthony Patch, too, corresponds in several important respects to characters who appear in Mencken's
tableau of democracy. Anthony is in revolt against his grandfather: "He's a pious ass—" says Anthony, "a chickenbrain."
Thus he seems to fit into the pattern of a typical Fitzgerald
theme—the Revolt of Youth. But if ever there were a bloodless revolution it is Anthony's. His protest against the older
generation is so lacking in vigor, his claims to independence
so feeble, that he seems markedly unlike Fitzgerald's other
heroes. The reason may be found in Fitzgerald's efforts to
make Anthony conform to Mencken's definition of the American *intelligentsia*, as already noted; a class typified, in
Mencken's words, by "a highly self-conscious and insipid
correctness, a bloodless respectability." Whatever the defects of Fitzgerald's first novel, *This Side of Paradise*, Amory
Blaine displayed an independence of spirit and a healthy
defiance of worn-out values that understandably captured
the imagination of his readers. Anthony Patch has no such
strength and no such appeal to the imagination. Anthony's
hopes for accomplishing anything at all, in fact, depend entirely upon his inheriting Adam Patch's fortune.

Deprived of this great expectation halfway through the novel, and having dissipated his own resources in a series of reckless and expensive drinking bouts, Anthony Patch begins his social and spiritual deterioration. He tries his hand unsuccessfully at selling stock in the absurd "Heart Talks" enterprise, an episode that gives Fitzgerald an opportunity to construct as effective a satire on the "go-getter" as anything in Sinclair Lewis. By this time Anthony and his once-beautiful wife have become accustomed to a series of moves into progressively poorer neighborhoods, a dwindling number of old friends and acquaintances, and an increasing resignation to failure and despair. Anthony takes refuge in drink and in the comradeship of anonymous drifters in a neighborhood bar, and Fitzgerald makes good use of these gloomy circumstances to suggest the true extent of Anthony's social misfortunes. "He hated to be sober," Fitzgerald tells us:

> It made him conscious of the people around him, of that air of struggle, of greedy ambition, of hope more sordid than despair, of incessant passage up and down, which in every metropolis is most in evidence in the unstable middle class. Unable to live with the rich he thought that his next choice would have been to live with the very poor. Anything was better than this cup of perspiration and tears.

At the same time Fitzgerald has Anthony reflect on the subject of aristocracy in a conversation with one of Gloria's friends, Muriel Kane:

> "You talk as if you and Gloria were in the middle classes," [Muriel said].
> "Why pretend we're not? I hate people who claim to be great aristocrats when they can't even keep up the appearances of it."
> "Do you think a person has to have money to be aristocratic?"

Muriel . . . the horrified democrat . . . !

"Why, of course. Aristocracy's only an admission that certain traits which we call fine—courage and honor and beauty and all that sort of thing—can best be developed in a favorable environment, where you don't have the warpings of ignorance and necessity."

It is such commentary, sprinkled throughout *The Beautiful and Damned,* that gives the novel its acute social awareness. Not that the intention of the foregoing passage is easy to pin down; but if I read it correctly Fitzgerald here approaches the high point of his irony and perception in the novel. Anthony Patch at first fancies himself an aristocrat-intellectual, an assumption based upon his independent income and his connection with Adam Patch. But Fitzgerald's treatment of Anthony and his grandfather indicates that there is nothing of the true aristocrat about either one of them. Hence Anthony's conversation with Muriel Kane touches upon one of the central themes of the book—America's illusion that wealth alone can produce those "certain traits which we call fine—courage and honor and beauty and all that sort of thing."

This is the very illusion that H. L. Mencken had been so conscientious in exposing. In an essay that appeared in 1919 (*Prejudices: First Series*) Mencken observed:

> The thing to blame, of course, is our lack of an intellectual aristocracy—sound in its information, skeptical in its habit of mind, and, above all, secure in its position and authority. Every other civilized country has such an aristocracy. It is the natural corrective of enthusiasms from below. It is hospitable to ideas, but as adamant against crazes. It stands against the pollution of logic by emotion, the sophistication of evidence to the glory of God. But in America there is nothing of the sort. On the one hand there is the populace—perhaps more powerful here, more capable of putting its

idiotic ideas into execution, than anywhere else—and surely
more eager to follow platitudinous messiahs. On the other
hand there is the ruling plutocracy—ignorant, hostile to inquiry, tyrannical in the exercise of its power, suspicious of
ideas of whatever sort. In the middle ground there is little
save an indistinct herd of intellectual eunuchs, chiefly
professors—often quite as stupid as the plutocracy and always in great fear of it. When it produces a stray rebel he
goes over to the mob; there is no place for him within his
own order.

These remarks contain the germ of Fitzgerald's novel:
they not only define the tone of disenchantment, they also
predict the general social scheme of *The Beautiful and
Damned*. Old Adam Patch represents Mencken's "ruling
plutocracy—ignorant, hostile to inquiry, etc." Anthony figures as a type of Mencken's "intellectual eunuchs" in the
middle ground—the stray rebel who eventually goes over to
the mob. The "unstable middle class"—which Anthony fears
and detests—is patterned after Mencken's "idiotic" populace.
It is one of the imaginative features of *The Beautiful and
Damned* that Fitzgerald's protagonist consecutively occupies
all three positions defined in Mencken's candid portrayal
of American society.

The emphasis of the story, however, is on the decline of
the hero, whose deterioration is made more perspicuous by
the ascent of Joseph Bloeckman, the Jewish motion-picture
entrepreneur whose gradual attainment of wealth, position,
and respectability provides a dissonant counterpoint to
Anthony's increasing hopelessness. Anthony Patch's attitude
toward Bloeckman consists of a deepening hostility and
snobbish resentment of the "established order" to intrusion
by the parvenu: the Jew, as we shall see in a later chapter,
was to many writers of the nineteen-twenties the representative par excellence of the postwar assault on the upper social

classes. "The war overthrew the old ruling caste of the land," Mencken asserts in an essay written in 1919, "and gave over control of things to upstarts from the lowest classes—shady Jews, snuffling Methodists, prehensile commercial gents, disgusting demagogues, all sorts of self-seeking adventurers." Anthony's dismayed observations, halfway through *The Beautiful and Damned,* reveal a close affinity with Mencken's diagnosis:

> Down in a tall busy street he read a dozen Jewish names on a line of stores; in the door of each stood a dark little man watching the passers from intent eyes—eyes gleaming with suspicion, with pride, with clarity, with cupidity, with comprehension. New York—he could not dissociate it now from the slow, upward creep of this people—the little stores, growing, expanding, consolidating, moving, watched over with hawk's eyes and a bee's attention to detail—they slathered out on all sides. It was impressive—in perspective it was tremendous.
>
> Gloria's voice broke in with strange appropriateness upon his thoughts.
>
> "I wonder where Bloeckman's been this summer."

Yet there is no malice in Fitzgerald's portrait of Joseph Bloeckman, who is treated in the novel as a social phenomenon neither to be condemned nor admired, a faintly ironic comment on social possibilities in America. Bloeckman was born in Munich, came to the United States as a young man, started his career as a peanut vendor in a traveling circus, rose to the position of manager of a side show and later of a vaudeville house, then invested in motion pictures when that industry was still in its infancy, and through good luck and perseverance attained some success and importance as a film producer. When Anthony first meets him, Bloeckman is "underdone . . . boiled looking," and Anthony responds to the man's social overtures with "a faint and ironic chill."

But later on Bloeckman reappears as a man of considerable substance, well dressed, obviously prospering, no longer eager to ingratiate himself: "The boiled look was gone, he seemed 'done' at last." And: "Anthony no longer felt a correct superiority in his presence." Toward the end of the novel, Mr. Bloeckman has become Mr. Black; he is now less a Jewish businessman than a seemingly established member of America's respectable upper middle class; and Anthony reflects, somewhat bitterly, that in Bloeckman-Black's manner "there was perceptibly more assurance that the fine things of the world were his by a natural and inalienable right." A hard fact for Anthony Patch to accept, even though it represents a fundamental American assumption, it is made more difficult by Anthony's recognition at the time that he himself has sunk to the lowest ragged edges of society.

Bloeckman is a more solidly conceived fictional character than either Anthony or Gloria Patch, about whom the author appears to be confused throughout most of the novel. Fitzgerald seems unable to decide whether his hero and heroine are attractive and glamorous or pitiful and undeserving of our sympathy. The final episode of the novel, as James E. Miller has pointed out, is an instance of this confusion. Here Fitzgerald's treatment of Anthony's responsibility for his actions contradicts our understanding of the hero's weakness and self-indulgence throughout. In the final chapters of *The Beautiful and Damned* Anthony Patch has abandoned all his earlier attempts to maintain the appearance of an "aristocrat." He has cut himself off from former friends; he has no income and cares little to improve his prospects; he has become an alcoholic and has even on one occasion been beaten and left to spend the night in the gutter. As a final excess, Fitzgerald has Anthony suffer a nervous breakdown and enter second childhood.

But in the midst of these melodramatic afflictions Anthony

is informed that the long litigation over his grandfather's will has been terminated. Anthony has won; he is now sole possessor of the Patch millions. The last scene shows Anthony congratulating himself on his good fortune and his endurance in the face of past difficulties (though what this "endurance" consists of Fitzgerald has failed to say). At this point in the novel it is uncertain where Fitzgerald's sympathies lie: is Anthony still misguided, full of illusions about himself, pathetic in his conception of his "victory"? Or is he truly the hero who has suffered and triumphed?

> [Anthony] was concerned with a series of reminiscences, much as a general might look back upon a successful campaign and analyze his victories. He was thinking of the hardships, the insufferable tribulations he had gone through. They had tried to penalize him for the mistakes of his youth. He had been exposed to ruthless misery, his very craving for romance had been punished, his friends had deserted him—even Gloria had turned against him. He had been alone, alone—facing it all.
>
> Only a few months before people had been urging him to give in, to submit to mediocrity, to go to work. But he had known that he was justified in his way of life—and he stuck it out staunchly. . . .
>
> Great tears stood in his eyes, and his voice was tremulous as he whispered to himself.
>
> "I showed them," he was saying. "It was a hard fight, but I didn't give up and I came through."

Fitzgerald's problems in presenting Anthony and Gloria Patch were of course formidable. No doubt part of his intention was to portray them, and the society above and below them, as puppets in a Menckenian social drama. Thus, he could make use of material picked up (if not thoroughly digested) from H. L. Mencken by his commentary, through Anthony, on the American *intelligentsia;*

through Adam Patch, on Comstockery and the American plutocracy; and through various characters and situations, on American social instability. But Fitzgerald also meant to emphasize Anthony and Gloria Patch's dedication to pleasure and to their own attractiveness as almost the only value they care to embrace. The result is that Fitzgerald makes more than a fair demand upon the reader's patience; one finds it difficult at best to become interested in the destiny of protagonists who, as Maxwell Geismar notes, have little or no character.

At the same time, Fitzgerald's sympathies, unlike Mencken's, are at least partially involved with the Patches' way of life, and his intention to depict the romance of idle dissipation interferes with his intention to be iconoclastic in the fashion of his mentor. Again and again in *The Beautiful and Damned* one senses Fitzgerald's confusion: Anthony Patch is supposed to represent a satirical thrust at an American type defined by Mencken; but Anthony is also the embodiment of Fitzgerald's yearning after sophistication. Thus, there is a division, as pronounced as that felt by Sinclair Lewis in his depiction of Babbitt, in Fitzgerald's attitude toward his protagonist. Apparently the materials and perspectives Fitzgerald derived from Mencken during this period were uncongenial to his own most deeply held convictions; or perhaps he had not yet achieved the maturity and experience necessary to transmute them satisfactorily into a work of fiction. In any case *The Beautiful and Damned* provides us with a picture of American society that lacks the clarity and vigor of Mencken's unequivocal assaults against the same fortress. Seen in this light the weaknesses and inconsistencies of *The Beautiful and Damned* emerge in high relief. Fitzgerald's impulse was obviously toward a fictional complexity and sophistication which he could not effectively render at this stage in his development.

But this is not to say that the novel is an artistic failure. Certainly *The Beautiful and Damned* is in many respects a solid achievement; like Edith Wharton's *The House of Mirth*, which it resembles in many ways (and upon which Fitzgerald drew for his portrait of Joseph Bloeckman), it defines for us the painful experience of an individual at odds with the prevailing mores of his time and place; and more important, it exhibits those social mores in something approaching the fullness of life. Had H. L. Mencken played no part in the conception of Fitzgerald's second novel, it might have been more consistent, less confused in its presentation of character; but it would certainly not have been so ambitious or so broad in scope. Mencken deepened Fitzgerald's understanding of American society; and what Fitzgerald learned from his involvement with social criticism in *The Beautiful and Damned* would be artistically realized in the perfection of *The Great Gatsby* and the fullness and depth of *Tender Is the Night*.

CHAPTER IV

Ring Lardner

> "For a year and a half, the writer of this appreciation was Ring Lardner's most familiar companion. . . ."
>
> —FITZGERALD IN "RING"

Fitzgerald's attitude toward Ring Lardner is in some respects puzzling. There can be no doubt that he admired Lardner and had deep respect and affection for the man. Fitzgerald saw him as "proud, shy, solemn, shrewd, polite, brave, kind, merciful, honorable"—"a great and good American" with an abundance of "noble dignity." These are the words Fitzgerald used in the memorial tribute I have referred to in an earlier chapter, the prose elegy that evoked so warm and emotional a response from Fitzgerald's friends. That response might well suggest to us the accuracy of Fitzgerald's comments on Lardner and his intimate understanding of Lardner's character.

But Fitzgerald's essay also stresses Lardner's artistic limitations. Fitzgerald believed that Lardner had failed to fulfill his promise, that "whatever Ring's achievement was, it fell far short of the achievement he was capable of." The reasons for this failure, according to Fitzgerald, were rather complicated: first of all, early in his career Lardner had adopted a "cynical attitude" toward his work; he simply refused to think that he had any great or important stories to tell. This attitude, Fitzgerald suggests, was partially temperamental; Lardner had assumed "a habit of silence. . . . He had agreed with himself to speak only a small portion of his mind." But Lardner's cynicism, Fitzgerald believed, was also the product of his early experiences as a sports reporter:

> During those years, when most men of promise achieve an adult education, if only in the school of war, Ring moved in the company of a few dozen illiterates playing a boy's game. A boy's game, with no more possibilities in it than a boy could master, a game bounded by walls which kept out novelty or danger, change or adventure. This material, the observation of it under such circumstances, was the text of Ring's schooling during the most formative period of the mind. A writer can spin on about his adventures after thirty, after forty, after fifty, but the criteria by which these adventures are weighed and valued are irrevocably settled at the age of twenty-five. However deeply Ring might cut into it, his cake had exactly the diameter of Frank Chance's diamond.

What, then, with these limitations, had Lardner accomplished? "There is *You Know Me, Al,* and there are about a dozen wonderful short stories . . . and there is some of the most uproarious and inspired nonsense since Lewis Carroll. Most of the rest is mediocre stuff, with flashes, and I would do Ring a disservice to suggest it should be set upon an altar and worshipped. . . ."

If there is more than a grain of truth in all this, there is also a large measure of injustice to Lardner. The man who "might have done much more" did, after all, a great deal; and Fitzgerald's emphasis upon the limited volume of Lardner's enduring work detracts notice from the force which that small body of fiction exerted upon American readers and writers. The impression Fitzgerald creates, in other words, is misleading not for what it says, but for what it omits about Lardner's true stature. Maxwell Geismar has written that Ring Lardner helped to change the currents of our literature. Of this there can be no doubt; Lardner's influence was far-reaching and pervasive. His themes anticipate those used time after time by the novelists and storytellers who succeeded him; writers as diverse as Sinclair Lewis and Ernest Hemingway in the twenties—as well as James Thurber, Thomas Wolfe, and James T. Farrell afterwards—are in his debt. Perhaps Fitzgerald was too close to his subject, in 1933, to see Ring Lardner's achievement in perspective; in this case, as in so many others, detachment might well play a decisive part. Still, Fitzgerald's underestimation of Lardner is difficult to understand. For Lardner exerted a significant influence on *The Great Gatsby*, Fitzgerald's most perfectly realized work of fiction.

Furthermore, Fitzgerald's notion of Lardner's "schooling" stands in need of correction. Baseball might well be a boy's game for those who take it as such—which Lardner certainly did not. Instead he used the ball park as an arena in which the human drama—at least in some of its comic and absurd aspects—is enacted. Fitzgerald's comment that Lardner, during his formative years, "moved in the company of a few dozen illiterates" is also a distortion, if we accept his association with such men as "the text of Ring's schooling." Baseball and baseball players represented Lardner's early material; but his attitudes toward his material, and his skill in representing it, were developed elsewhere. In fact, Lardner's early education was not far different from Fitzgerald's writing apprenticeship at Princeton. His university was *The Chicago Tribune,* where for nine years (from 1908 to 1919, with an interruption of two and a half years) he was employed as a columnist and sports reporter, and where he met a number of professional associates who helped shape his career and writing style. These men—humorists, reporters, and sports writers such as Charlie Dryden, Hugh Fullerton, Harry Leon Wilson, and Hugh Keogh—taught Lardner valuable lessons. Of minor but original talent, they helped to establish the direction of his prose a few years after he arrived in Chicago.

In addition, Lardner gained useful experience in writing his column "In the Wake of the News," which soon became one of the most popular of the *Tribune's* features. Baseball news occupied him only part of the time; he frequently did experimental pieces—verse, vignettes, short dramas, and letters in dialect, all of which look forward to the work of the mature artist. What the *Nassau Lit* was to Fitzgerald, "In the Wake of the News" was to Lardner: during the crucial apprenticeship period of their careers both writers found an ever-increasing number of enthusiastic readers and a ready testing ground for their talents. The "Wake" column not only helped Lardner develop the writing style that was to be the foundation of his art; it also gave him the opportunity, thanks to the liberal policy of the *Tribune* editors, to expand his interests, to try his hand at shrewd and cynical interpretations of American character types and a wide range of topical themes. In the end, the "Wake" was a steppingstone from obscurity to fame, and from journalism to serious art. By 1919, the transition was complete.

For several years Lardner had been contemplating a move to the East. Many of his newspaper friends had left Chicago to take jobs in and around New York, and he himself had long felt an impulse to follow their example, partly to satisfy a growing interest in the theater. When a newspaper syndicate in New York offered him a large salary to conduct a weekly column, Lardner accepted the offer and made it an occasion for leaving the Midwest. In 1919, he and his family moved to Greenwich, Connecticut ("The Young Immigrunts" is a memorably comic record of that trip). A year later they moved once more—this time to stay only a few months—to Garden City, Long Island; and then, in 1921, to Great Neck, Long Island, where they remained until 1928.

Meanwhile, Fitzgerald had been enjoying the success of *This Side of Paradise*, and with Zelda had spent the early years of the new decade in hard work and restless travel. The Fitzgeralds had come to New York early in 1920; after a few months they moved to Westport, Connecticut, for the summer and fall of that year; the following spring they sojourned briefly in England; on their return to America they stayed for a year in St. Paul; and in the autumn of 1922 they came back to New York to settle for a year and a half in Great Neck. Here Fitzgerald and Lardner were neighbors, and they soon became close friends. Lardner was thirty-seven; Fitzgerald was twenty-six.

In his biography of Ring Lardner, Donald Elder has described the two writers' frequent convivial evenings, which were held sometimes at Fitzgerald's house, sometimes at Lardner's. They often sat up through the night drinking and talking, alone or with a few friends; they read and discussed the same magazines and books, among which was Gertrude Stein's *Three Lives*, which Lardner read on Fitzgerald's recommendation. At the end of these evenings, with the sun streaming through the parlor windows, Lardner would get up and say: "Well, I guess the children have

left for school by this time—I might as well go home."
Lardner was working hard during this period—he had two
syndicate features, several magazine articles in progress,
and numerous fragments of plays to be completed. Fitzgerald, who had a great deal of respect for Lardner's
talent, felt certain that Lardner was wasting himself on
these insignificant efforts. He was afraid that Lardner was
inadvertently suppressing his real genius.[1]

Fitzgerald's concern was genuine; and he urged his friend
to apply himself (as Fitzgerald recalled years later in
"Ring") to something sustained and significant:

> The present writer once suggested to him that he organize
> some *cadre* within which he could adequately display his
> talents, suggesting that it should be something deeply per-
> sonal, and something on which Ring could take his time,
> but he dismissed the idea lightly; he was a disillusioned
> idealist but he had served his Fates well, and no other ones
> could be casually created for him—"This is something that
> can be printed," he reasoned; "this, however, belongs with
> that bunch of stuff that can never be written."

But if Lardner could not be persuaded to undertake new
and different projects, he did respond to another suggestion
Fitzgerald made in 1923. Lardner was enjoying great
popularity as a syndicated newspaper columnist and as the
author of "The Young Immigrunts" and the earlier *You
Know Me, Al*. He was also well known to readers of the
Saturday Evening Post and *Cosmopolitan* as a frequent con-
tributor of humorous and satirical short stories. But he had
never collected any of his stories between hard covers; and
Fitzgerald, hoping to attract critical attention to this area of
Lardner's fiction, proposed such a collection both to Lardner
and to Scribner's. The result was *How To Write Short*

[1] *Ring Lardner* (New York: Doubleday and Co., Inc., 1956), pp.
183-185.

Stories, which sold extremely well and at the same time established Lardner as a serious artist in the short-story form. Fitzgerald had not only originated the idea for the collection; he had supplied the title and assisted in the selection of stories.

Furthermore, shortly before the appearance of *How To Write Short Stories* Fitzgerald persuaded Maxwell Perkins at Scribner's to reissue several of Lardner's works that for some years had been out of print. Consequently, in 1925, Scribner's brought out *You Know Me, Al, Gullible's Travels,* and *The Big Town.* These volumes, together with *How To Write Short Stories,* helped Lardner attain a greater and more enthusiastic following than ever before. The critics, too, were impressed; and Lardner was on his way to undreamed-of recognition. By 1929, with the publication of *Round Up* (which contained all of Lardner's best stories up to that time), more than one reviewer was earnestly comparing Ring Lardner with Chekhov and Shakespeare.

Fitzgerald may well have underestimated his influence on Lardner. The younger man was eager for Lardner to try his hand at writing a novel; this Lardner did not do, but in the years following his period of close association with Fitzgerald he turned more and more frequently to the third-person short story as a vehicle. Without the critical recognition of the middle twenties, and without Fitzgerald's repeated suggestions that he try something beyond his customary range and style, Lardner might never have written "The Love Nest," "There Are Smiles," or "Old Folks' Christmas."

In the spring of 1924, Fitzgerald left Great Neck to travel abroad and to finish *The Great Gatsby,* which he had begun a few months earlier. He left Lardner to look after such details as the renting of the house in Great Neck, the repairs required by the new tenants, and the sometimes precarious state of Fitzgerald's account at the Great Neck bank: Lardner covered his friend's overdrafts by hastily depositing the rent from Fitzgerald's tenants; on one occasion he covered one of Fitzgerald's checks out of his own pocket.

In the meantime the two friends carried on a lively correspondence. "To no one else outside his family," Lardner's biographer tells us, "did Ring write such affectionate, trusting, and revealing letters." Lardner kept Fitzgerald informed on the social life of New York and Long Island, the gossip that was so much a part of the frequent parties he attended, and his own professional activities. I reproduce here a few excerpts from Lardner's letters to Fitzgerald that are characteristic of his tone and interests during this period.

March 24, 1925
We had a dinner party at our little nest two weeks ago; the guests were the Ray Longs, the Grantland Rices, June Walker, and Frank Crowninshield. As place cards for Ray, Crownie, and Grant, we had, respectively, covers of Cosmopolitan, Vanity Fair and The American Golfer, but this didn't seem to make any impression on June and right after the soup she began knocking Condé Nast in general and his alleged snobbishness in particular. Finally Crownie butted in to defend him and June said, "What do you know about him?" "I live with him," said Crownie. "What for?" said June. "Well," said Crownie, "I happen to be editor of one of his magazines, Vanity Fair." "Oh!" said June. "That's my favorite magazine! And I hate most magazines! For instance, I wouldn't be seen with Cosmopolitan." After the loud laughter had subsided, I explained to her that Ray was editor of Cosmopolitan. "I'm always making breaks," she said, "and I guess this is one of my unlucky evenings. I suppose that if I said what I think of William R. Hearst, I'd find that even he has a friend here or something." [Grantland Rice wrote for the Hearst newspapers.]

1925

Some of the Algonquin bunch was sort of riding Michael Arlen, I don't know why. Anyway, when Edna Ferber was introduced to him, she said: "Why, Mr. Arlen, you look almost like a woman!" "So do you, Miss Ferber," was Michael's reply.

May, 1926

Red Lewis got the [Pulitzer] Prize with "Arrowsmith" and turned it down. I can see his point. I am against all that kind of stuff, meaning the Pulitzer awards and the All American football team and "The Best Short Stories of so-and-so," even when Mr. O'Brien honors me with a place or three or four stars in the last named.

In the spring of 1925, with *The Great Gatsby* about to be released, Lardner reported:

I read Mr. F's book (in page proofs) at one sitting and liked it enormously, particularly the description of Gatsby's home and his party, and the party in the apartment in New York. It sounds as if Mr. F. must have attended a party or two during his metropolitan career. The plot held my interest, too, and I found no tedious moments. Altogether I think it's the best thing you've done since Paradise.

On the other hand, I acted as volunteer proof reader and gave Max a brief list of what I thought were errata. On page 31 and 46 you spoke of the newsstand on the *lower level* of the Pennsylvania station. There ain't any lower level on that station and I suggested substitute terms for same. On page 82 you had the guy driving his car under the elevated at Astoria, which isn't Astoria, but Long Island City. On page 118 you had a tide in Lake Superior and on page 209 you had the Chicago, Milwaukee and St. Paul running out of the Lasalle Street Station. These things are trivial, but some of the critics pick on trivial errors for lack of anything else to pick on.

Some of these errors of detail Fitzgerald corrected at Lardner's suggestion; others he let stand.

When Fitzgerald returned to America at the end of 1926 he immediately accepted an offer from Hollywood to work on a film script, and he spent the next several months on the West Coast. Thereafter, up to the time of Lardner's death in 1933, Fitzgerald stayed successively in Montgomery, Alabama; Wilmington, Delaware; and outside Baltimore, Maryland. Lardner, in the meantime, had settled in East Hampton, Long Island. Thus separated, and caught up each in his own personal and professional problems, the two friends saw little of each other during these years.

The letters from Lardner, however, continued. From time to time he wrote to Fitzgerald about his own projects; and on one occasion he sent an ironic inquiry concerning the novel Fitzgerald had been struggling to complete for five years:

> Feb. 27, 1930
> I hear from Max Perkins that your book is nearly finished. What are you calling it, The Encyclopedia Britannica?

At the time this was written, Lardner was suffering from various physical ailments (an examination in 1926 revealed that he had tuberculosis) and from the ever-deepening mental depression that drove him into long lapses of silence and repeated periods of heavy drinking. From 1930 until his death three years later, he fought a losing battle against ill-health and despondency. Much of his time was spent in hospitals and in trips to California and Arizona, where he hoped to find rest and at least partial recovery. More and more he withdrew into himself, maintaining contact with only a few close friends and members of his immediate family.

Fitzgerald saw Lardner for the last time in 1931, when

the latter was in the early stages of his final decline. "He looked already like a man on his deathbed," Fitzgerald recalled in "Ring." "It was terribly sad to see that six feet three inches of kindness stretched out ineffectual in the hospital room. His fingers trembled with a match, the tight skin on his handsome skull was marked as a mask of misery and nervous pain." Two years later Maxwell Perkins wrote Fitzgerald: "I think things are bad with Ring. I hate to inquire. He is at Easthampton and nobody ever seems to see him." A month later Lardner was dead.

At the time, Fitzgerald was deeply involved in writing the final chapters of *Tender Is the Night,* the novel he had been working on for eight years. Perkins wrote asking for Fitzgerald's assistance in the preparation of a "memorial" collection of Lardner's work. The volume, Perkins suggested, would need an introduction "by someone really appreciative of [Lardner] as a writer, and at the same time knew him well as a man. . . . Would you be willing to undertake it?" Perkins also asked if Fitzgerald could supply a picture of Lardner for this volume. "I would almost rather have it after the Great Neck days [i.e., after 1928] because, although he did look terribly gaunt and ill, even before he went to the hospital, I do think that you could see better what a remarkable creature he was then."

Fitzgerald did for a time contemplate editing the collection Perkins had suggested and he exchanged letters with Lardner's son John, asking for advice on the selection of material. But Fitzgerald's commitment to his own work was pressing, and eventually the task of editing a posthumous Lardner volume was undertaken by Gilbert Seldes.

The fictional character Abe North in *Tender Is the Night* is Fitzgerald's portrait of Ring Lardner, and perhaps the most eloquent reminder of the deep impression Lardner made on the younger writer. Fitzgerald emphasized Abe

North's failure to fulfill an early artistic promise, charac-
terizing him as "a musician who after a brilliant and precocious start had composed nothing for seven years." North
also has lost all interest in his work, in his friends, and in
life itself:

> "I used to think until you're eighteen nothing matters,"
> said Mary.
> "That's right," Abe agreed. "And afterward it's the same
> way."

> "The afternoon you took me to that funny ball—you know,
> St. Genevieve's—" [Abe] began.
> "I remember. It was fun, wasn't it?" [said Nicole.]
> "No fun for me. I haven't had fun seeing you this time.
> I'm tired of you both, but it doesn't show because you're
> even more tired of me—you know what I mean. If I had any
> enthusiasm, I'd go on to new people."
> There was a rough nap on Nicole's velvet gloves as she
> slapped him back:
> "Seems rather foolish to be unpleasant, Abe. Anyhow
> you don't mean that. I can't see why you've given up about
> everything."
> Abe considered, trying hard not to cough or blow his
> nose.
> "I suppose I got bored; and then it was such a long way
> to go back in order to get anywhere."

Abe, in fact, has lost interest in everything but drink. And
though the qualities that endeared Lardner to Fitzgerald
are still visible, Abe North's physical debility and his spiritual despair have overwhelmed other aspects of his character
(at times in his description of Abe North, Fitzgerald uses
the same telling details he applied to Lardner in "Ring"):

> "Tired of women's worlds," [Abe] spoke up suddenly.
> "Then why don't you make a world of your own?"
> [Nicole said.]

"Tired of friends. The thing is to have sycophants."
Nicole tried to force the minute hand around on the station
clock, but, "You agree?" he demanded.

"I am a woman and my business is to hold things together."

"My business is to tear them apart."

"When you get drunk you don't tear anything apart except yourself," she said, cold now, and frightened and
unconfident. The station was filling but no one she knew
came. After a moment her eyes fell gratefully on a tall girl
with straw hair like a helmet, who was dropping letters in
the mail slot.

"A girl I have to speak to, Abe. Abe, wake up! You fool!"

Patiently Abe followed her with his eyes. The woman
turned in a startled way to greet Nicole, and Abe recognized her as some one he had seen around Paris. He
took advantage of Nicole's absence to cough hard and
retchingly into his handkerchief, and to blow his nose loud.
The morning was warmer and his underwear was soaked
with sweat. His fingers trembled so violently that it took
four matches to light a cigarette; it seemed absolutely
necessary to make his way into the buffet for a drink. . . .

The noble dignity of Abe's face took on a certain stub-
bornness. . . .

Dick laughed indulgently at Abe, whom he loved, and
in whom he had long lost hope. . . .

They stood in an uncomfortable little group weighted
down by Abe's gigantic presence: he lay athwart them like
the wreck of a galleon, dominating with his presence his
own weakness and self-indulgence, his narrowness and
bitterness. All of them were conscious of the solemn dignity
that flowed from him, of his achievement, fragmentary,
suggestive and surpassed. But they were frightened at his
survivant will, once a will to live, now become a will to die.

"Abe used to be so nice," Nicole told Rosemary. "So

nice. Long ago—when Dick and I were first married. If you had known him then. He'd come to stay with us for weeks and weeks and we scarcely knew he was in the house. Sometimes he'd play—sometimes he'd be in the library with a muted piano, making love to it by the hour—Dick, do you remember that maid? She thought he was a ghost and sometimes Abe used to meet her in the hall and moo at her, and it cost us a whole tea service once—but we didn't care."

"What did this to him?" [Rosemary] asked. "Why does he have to drink?"

Nicole shook her head right and left, disclaiming responsibility for the matter: "So many smart men go to pieces nowadays."

"And when haven't they?" Dick asked. "Smart men play close to the line because they have to—some of them can't stand it, so they quit."

Toward the end of the novel Fitzgerald has Dick Diver overhear the final and tragic chapter of his friend's history: Abe North has been beaten to death in a New York speakeasy. It is perhaps fortunate that Lardner did not live to read Fitzgerald's fictional interpretation of his character in *Tender Is the Night*. Years earlier Lardner had portrayed Zelda and Scott Fitzgerald as Cinderella and the Prince in one of his burlesque fairy tales.

Fitzgerald exaggerated Lardner's "deterioration" and underestimated (both in "Ring" and in *Tender Is the Night*) the quality and significance of the man's artistic achievement. "Am going on the water wagon from the first of February to the first of April," Fitzgerald wrote Maxwell Perkins early in 1933. "But don't tell Ernest [Hemingway] because he has long convinced himself that I am an incurable alcoholic. . . . I am *his* alcoholic just like Ring is mine. . . ." This is a revealing statement, and a clue to one of the basic elements in Fitzgerald's attitude toward his friend: Lardner was for Fitzgerald a man of gentle, affectionate, even noble character; but he was also a compulsive drinker and an artist who had realized only a small measure of his potential.

But it is important to understand that Fitzgerald felt not only sympathy with Lardner's drinking problem and (relative) artistic failure; he also felt a positive sense of identification with these unhappy tendencies in his friend's character. The man who in 1936 was to write with brutal frankness in "The Crack-Up" of his own deterioration saw in Ring Lardner a reflection of his own weakness, his own tendencies toward alcoholism, despair, and artistic failure. As a matter of fact, the portrait of Abe North in *Tender Is the Night* is extremely revealing as a comment on Fitzgerald himself. The description of the artist who "after a brilliant and precocious start had composed nothing for seven years" can apply as well to Fitzgerald (who at the time had not published a novel for several years) as to Lardner. Furthermore, Abe North's decline is a counterpoint to the decline of Dick Diver, the major figure in the novel and a character who bears more than an incidental resemblance to Fitzgerald. As Arthur Mizener, borrowing a phrase from Conrad, observes, North and Diver are "secret sharers." Here, then, was one of the foundations of the relationship between Lardner and Fitzgerald. It was part of Fitzgerald's deepest understanding of his friend: he saw in Lardner what he feared was happening to himself.

The two writers, however, had something in common that overshadowed even this major element in their relationship. They were practicing literary artists, and they consistently drew their inspiration from an awareness of current attitudes and events. In their works is reflected a profound interest in the ephemera of the nineteen-twenties—the fashions, fads, and popular enterprises of the day; but they also recorded more essential aspects of national experience—the rhythms of American speech, the patterns of contemporary behavior, the ethics of the moment, the tragedies. Fitzgerald and Lardner shared a fascination with America during one of the most dramatic periods in its history.

Donald Elder observes that Lardner and Fitzgerald were both "disabused in the same way, they had lost their beliefs, and their judgments on their times were basically the same." With this statement I am in complete accord, though there is much to be said concerning the two authors' different perspectives. Lardner's stories are humorous, ironic, at times fiercely pessimistic, and unequivocal in their intention and meaning. Fitzgerald's fiction, in contrast, is dominated by a romantic tone and emphasis and is frequently complicated by an ambiguity in the author's attitude toward his material. Yet time after time Fitzgerald and Lardner treat the same themes and subjects, and in their very best work they reach for, and arrive at, the same conclusions.

II

"Go to Florida—
"Where enterprise is enthroned—
"Where you sit and watch at twilight the fronds of the graceful palm, latticed against the fading gold of the sun-kissed sky—
"Where sun, moon and stars, at eventide, stage a welcome constituting the glorious galaxy of the firmament—
"Where the whispering breeze springs fresh from the lap of Caribbean and woos with elusive cadence like unto a mother's lullaby. . . ."

The above, written in 1925, is quoted in Frederick Lewis Allen's *Only Yesterday* as an example of the "unbuttoned rhetoric" inspired by the Florida real-estate boom. At the time the advertisement was written, the "great white Goddess of states" had become a center of feverish buying and selling and a source of enormous profits to the land speculators who swarmed within its borders. A few years earlier, on the eve of Coolidge prosperity, Florida had been a vacation playground for the rich; and its exotic attractions were well suited to the purposes of the popular fictionist. Fitzgerald no doubt sensed the romantic appeal of such a setting when in 1920 he wrote:

> This unlikely story begins on a sea that was a blue dream, as colorful as blue-silk stockings, and beneath a sky as blue as the irises of children's eyes. From the western half of the sky the sun was shying little golden disks at the sea— if you gazed intently enough you could see them skip from wave tip to wave tip until they joined a broad collar of golden coin that was collecting half a mile out and would eventually be a dazzling sunset. About half-way between the Florida shore and the golden collar a white steam-yacht, very young and graceful, was riding at anchor and under a blue and white awning aft a yellow-haired girl reclined in a wicker settee. . . .

The passage speaks for itself. For descriptive gaudiness Fitzgerald's prose outshines that of the public-relations promoter, pamphleteering at the height of the Florida boom. The story from which it is taken appeared in the *Saturday Evening Post* under the title "The Offshore Pirate," and concerns a handsome young man and a beautiful young girl who fall in love against a colorful backdrop of palms, lagoons, and crimson sunsets.[2]

Meanwhile, in 1917, Ring Lardner had documented his impressions of Florida's allure. The cynical narrator of "Gullible's Travels" had discovered a semitropical paradise that was relatively barren of enchantment:

[2] The passage from "The Offshore Pirate" is also cited by Henry Dan Piper in his unpublished doctoral dissertation (University of Pennsylvania, 1950), "Scott Fitzgerald and the Origins of the Jazz Age," p. 36. I have followed Piper's comments on the relation of "The Offshore Pirate" to the Florida boom.

They was about two dozen uniformed Ephs on the job to meet us. And when I seen 'em all grab for our baggage with one hand and hold the other out, face up, I knowed why they called it Palm Beach.

And while Fitzgerald's breathless youngsters cavort in a "shimmering channel" under a sky "shadowy blue and silver," Lardner's tourists are enjoying a unique sight-seeing excursion:

First, we went to St. George Street and visited the oldest house in the United States. Then we went to Hospital Street and seen the oldest house in the United States. Then we turned the corner and went down St. Francis Street and inspected the oldest house in the United States. Then we dropped into a soda fountain and I had an egg phosphate, made from the oldest egg in the Western Hemisphere. We passed up lunch and got into a carriage drawn by the oldest horse in Florida, and we rode through the country all afternoon and the driver told us some o' the oldest jokes in the book.

Later, Lardner's hero and heroine take a ride along the boardwalk in a vehicle native to Florida resorts: "It was part bicycle, part go-cart and part African." They wind up the day in the hotel ballroom:

I bet you any amount you name that the Castles in their whole life haven't danced together as much as I and the Missus did at Palm Beach. I'd of gave five dollars if even one o' the waiters had took her offen my hands for one dance. But I knowed that if I made the offer public they'd of been a really serious quarrel between us instead o' just the minor brawls occasioned by steppin' on each other's feet.

Fitzgerald's Palm Beach (in a later story) "sprawls plump and opulent between the sparkling sapphire of Lake Worth, flawed here and there by house-boats at anchor, and the great turquoise bar of the Atlantic Ocean." His young couple, dissatisfied with bridge-playing at the Everglades Club, wander out to a moonlit beach:

> "Darling, darling. . . ."
> They embraced recklessly, passionately, in a shadow. . . .

The treatment of Florida is hardly of major significance in the fiction of Lardner and Fitzgerald; yet the contrast is revealing. Here we find Fitzgerald exploiting every possibility for glamor—and for romance, in the popular sense of the term. And here we find Lardner's characteristic cynicism, his instinctive grasp of the ridiculous, and his penchant for the wisecrack.[3] These differences are apparent in other themes and subjects which Fitzgerald and Lardner treated.

We find the same contrast, for example, in the two authors' attitudes toward another, more significant phenomenon of the twenties—the Revolt (as it has been called) of the Younger Generation. The actions of Fitzgerald's flappers dramatically reflect that spirited change in the behavior of the American adolescent. The flapper was, for one thing, contemptuous of the older generation. Witness the following interview, which takes place between Ardita Farnam, the heroine of "The Offshore Pirate," and her middle-aged uncle:

> "Ardita!" said the gray-haired man sternly.
> Ardita uttered a small sound indicating nothing.
> "Ardita!" he repeated. "Ardita!"
> Ardita raised the lemon languidly, allowing three words to slip out before it reached her tongue.
> "Oh, shut up."

[3] Other writers of the period also left impressions of Florida during the nineteen-twenties. See Thomas Wolfe, *Look Homeward, Angel* (New York, 1960), p. 133; and John Dos Passos, *U.S.A.* (New York, 1937), III, pp. 340-342.

"Ardita!"

"What?"

"Will you listen to me—or will I have to get a servant to hold you while I talk to you?"

"Put it in writing."

"Will you have the decency to close that abominable book and discard the damn lemon for two minutes?"

. . . "O-o-o-oh!" The cry was wrung from Ardita with the agony of a lost soul. "Will you stop boring me! Will you go 'way! Will you jump overboard and drown! Do you want me to throw this book at you!"

"If you dare do any—"

Smack! The Revolt of the Angels sailed through the air, missed its target by the length of a short nose, and bumped cheerfully down the companionway.

The gray-haired man made an instinctive step backward and then two cautious steps forward. Ardita jumped to her five feet four and stared at him defiantly, her gray eyes blazing.

"Keep off!"

"How dare you!"

"Because I darn please!"

"You've grown unbearable! Your disposition—"

"You've made me that way! No child ever has a bad disposition unless it's her family's fault! Whatever I am, you did it!"

The flapper, having thus explained away the causes of her petulance, turns her attention to another, more agreeable subject—herself. Fitzgerald frequently presents her as quite conscious of her physical charms and flawless grooming, as in the following excerpt from "May Day":

She thought of her own appearance. Her bare arms and shoulders were powdered to a creamy white. She knew they looked very soft and would gleam like milk against the black backs that were to silhouette them tonight. The hair-dressing had been a success; her reddish mass of hair was piled and crushed and creased to an arrogant marvel of mobile curves. Her lips were finely made of deep carmine; the irises of her eyes were delicate, breakable blue, like china eyes. She was a complete, infinitely delicate, quite perfect thing of beauty, flowing in an even line from a complex coiffure to two small feet. . . . She had never felt her own softness so much nor so enjoyed the whiteness of her own arms.

She is also reluctant to abandon her narcissistic pleasures for more adult pursuits, which she views with loathing:

"You know [says the Debutante of *This Side of Paradise*] I'm old in some ways—in others,—well, I'm just a little girl. I like sunshine and pretty things and cheerfulness—and I dread responsibility. I don't want to think about pots and kitchens and brooms. I want to worry whether my legs will get slick and brown when I swim in the summer."

And Gloria Gilbert, the heroine of *The Beautiful and Damned*, reflects:

"Marriage was created not to be a background but to need one. Mine is going to be outstanding. It can't, shan't be the setting—it's going to be the performance, the live, lovely, glamorous performance, and the world shall be the scenery. I refuse to dedicate my life to posterity. Surely one owes as much to the current generation as to one's unwanted children. What a fate—to grow rotund and unseemly, to lose my self-love, to think in terms of milk, oatmeal, nurse, diapers. . . . Dear little dream children, how much more beautiful you are, dazzling little creatures who flutter on golden, golden wings. . . ."

The flapper is also fickle and flirtatious, with an honest indifference to her most ardent devotees. Occasionally Fitzgerald has his heroines attempt to apologize for their fickleness, as if it were a failing; at the same time, this quality of character exerts a strong force of attraction on the young author. In "Winter Dreams" Judy Jones confesses to Dexter Green: "I don't know what's the matter with me. Last night I thought I was in love with a man and tonight I think I'm in love with you. . . ." Dexter's reaction to this is typical: "It seemed to him a beautiful and romantic thing to say. It was the exquisite excitability that for the moment he controlled and owned." [4] And Minnie Bibble, of "Basil and Cleopatra," pleads innocent of any responsibility for her lighthearted capriciousness: "Oh, Basil, am I just perfectly terrible? I never want to be mean to anybody; things just happen." After Minnie's all-covering evasion, Basil, we are told, "wanted to put his arm around her and tell her she was the most romantic person in the world. . . ."

But for all her coldness, inconstancy, and narcissism, Fitzgerald's flapper is amorous by nature; and she takes a keen delight in the pleasures of love—when those pleasures are limited, that is, to innocent kisses: "A woman," says Gloria Gilbert in *The Beautiful and Damned*, "should be able to kiss a man beautifully and romantically without any desire to be either his wife or his mistress."

But she must not be restricted, another of Fitzgerald's heroines makes clear, to one partner: "I've kissed dozens of men," boasts Rosaline Connage in *This Side of Paradise*. "I suppose I'll kiss dozens more."

It is probably true, as Fitzgerald himself claimed years later, that his depiction of the flapper was largely responsible for the popularity of his early novels and stories. And the composite portrait I have drawn above suggests his attitude toward the romantic figure he helped to create. As Paul Rosenfeld remarked in 1925, Fitzgerald did not recognize his characters for what they were; he invested them with the glamor with which they pathetically invested

[4] Fitzgerald apparently was unaware of the ironic insult to Dexter in Judy Jones's statement.

themselves. We might summarize Fitzgerald's attitude toward the flapper and all that she represented with a line spoken by Curtis Carlyle, the hero of "The Offshore Pirate":

> Suddenly against the golden furnace low in the east their two graceful figures melted into one, and he was kissing her spoiled young mouth.
> "It's a sort of glory," he murmured. . . .

To Ring Lardner it was a sort of abomination. In at least a few incisive and uncompromising sketches, Lardner deals cynically or satirically with those qualities of the flapper's character which enlisted Fitzgerald's admiration. Consider, for example, the story "I Can't Breathe," in which Lardner's adolescent heroine spends a two-week vacation tangling up her boy friends' lives. The story unfolds in the form of a diary kept by Lardner's flapper, who is as empty-headed as Fitzgerald's girls are insouciant:

> I am staying here at the Inn for two weeks with my Uncle Nat and Aunt Jule and I think I will keep a kind of diary while I am here to help pass the time and so I can have a record of things that happen though goodness knows there isn't lightly to anything happen, that is anything exciting with Uncle Nat and Aunt Jule making the plans as they are both at least 35 years old and maybe older.

Left to her own devices she trifles with one suitor who is staying at the Inn, corresponds with two others who are already making plans to marry her, and finally abandons all three for a returned ex-sweetheart who suddenly appears just as her vacation is drawing to a close. In the midst of these involvements Lardner's heroine reflects philosophically that in a world made over to her specifications she would be at liberty to marry all four of her admirers in succession:

Life is so hopeless and it could be so wonderful. For instance how heavenly it would be if I could marry Frank first and stay married to him five years and he would be the one who would take me to Hollywood and maybe we could go on parties with Norman Kerry and Jack Barrymore and Buster Collier and Marion Davies and Lois Moran.

And at the end of five years Frank could go into journalism and write novels and I would be only 23 and I could marry Gordon and he would be ready for another trip around the world and he could show me things better than someone who had never seen them before.

Gordon and I would separate at the end of five years and I would be 28 and I know of lots of women that never even got married the first time till they were 28 though I don't suppose that was their fault, but I would marry Walter then, for after all he is the one I really love and want to spend most of my life with and I wouldn't care whether he could dance or not when I was that old. Before long we would be as old as Uncle Nat and Aunt Jule and I certainly wouldn't want to dance at their age when all you can do is just hobble around the floor. But Walter is so wonderful as a companion and we would enjoy the same things and be pals and maybe we would begin to have children.

But that is all impossible though it wouldn't be if older people just had sense and would look at things the right way.

But "I Can't Breathe" is a relatively mild satire on the flapper Fitzgerald popularized. Another story, written in 1929, draws on a deeper vein of contempt. In "Old Folks' Christmas" Lardner systematically divests the Revolt of Youth of every particle of appeal.

Ted and Caroline Carter, the adolescents of "Old Folks' Christmas," were christened Junior and Grace. But "Junior had changed his name to Ted and Grace was now Caroline, and thus they insisted on being addressed, even by their parents." The youngsters, who have delayed their holiday homecoming from school, offer transparent alibis for their failure to arrive on schedule; but in fact Ted has been on a drunk, and his seventeen-year-old sister has probably kept some casual assignation en route. As soon as they arrive at the house they take afternoon naps, then a friend calls for them in his new roadster. Shortly after three the next morning the roadster returns; forty minutes later Caroline staggers up to bed, scarcely pausing to greet her parents, who have waited up. Ted comes in around dawn, hangs his hat and coat "carefully" on the hall floor and retires to his bedroom. The children spend Christmas morning recuperating and making plans to exchange the gifts that the Carters senior have carefully selected for them. Next they present their progenitors with two tickets to a stale Broadway musical for that evening—a convenient and respectable ruse for getting them out of the house. When Mr. and Mrs. Carter return late that night, they are greeted by a scene of devastation—the aftermath of the entertainment to which Ted and Caroline have treated their friends.

The tone Lardner maintains in "Old Folks' Christmas" is far from that of caricature: Ted and Caroline Carter are outwardly civil to, even thoughtful of, their parents. Without doubt their real-life counterparts existed in many American homes. Artistically Lardner is neither subtle nor profound here; but the story is still a penetrating commentary on the life of the times, and certainly one of the most individual and realistic treatments of a theme that engaged more than a few major writers of the period.[5]

Perhaps the comparison drawn above is not quite fair to Fitzgerald, whose young rebels accurately reflect the spirit and mood of their generation. In all justice, it must be ad-

[5] For an excellent summary of popular fictional treatments of the Younger Generation, see Frederick J. Hoffman, *The Twenties* (New York, 1955), pp. 86-100.

mitted that Fitzgerald's debutantes and playboys are no mere glamorized versions of Lardner's irresponsible adolescents. Almost invariably they act and speak out of a conviction that they are engaged in a kind of holy crusade for self-determination. The disregard for convention, the casual attitude toward admirers, the defiance of the older generation—all these are invested with the dignity Fitzgerald believed to be inherent in the Younger Generation's code of conduct. Fitzgerald always makes an attempt (sometimes bathetic, but in any case consistent) to portray the attitudes and actions of youth as earnest and intensely felt. None of these distinguishing qualities apply to Lardner's undisciplined children. Lacking in any code save that of self-interest, they are frankly detestable.[6]

Still another theme, more important and more pervasive than those already considered, attracted the attention of Lardner and Fitzgerald. Both writers manifest a profound interest in the social disruption that followed World War I and that attended the prosperity of the Harding-Coolidge era. It was against this background, in fact, that Ring Lardner projected his most incisive studies of American life. His best stories record the emergence of a parvenu class, a society which finds itself, somewhat to its own bewilderment, suddenly affluent, and therefore—according to one of the basic assumptions of democracy—blessed with the freedom to claim status. Lardner's target is the pretensions of his class; he misses no opportunity to expose the ludicrous disappointments and humiliations that await the socially uninitiated.

Fitzgerald's treatment of this theme differs, of course, in

[6] There are a few exceptions: see the healthy youngsters in "The Young Immigrunts" and the daring and carefree Edith Dole of "There Are Smiles."

its particulars; his would-be aristocrats are conscious of what they are trying to achieve and acutely aware of their failures, while Lardner's are relatively callous and unperceptive. Fitzgerald's eager protagonists suffer the consequences of their self-imposed social displacement: they lose dignity or youthful optimism, or vitality, or life itself; Lardner's interlopers are incapable of any such noble distress. Fitzgerald's tone is tragic, Lardner's satiric. Lardner's cynicism and his detachment are everywhere apparent; Fitzgerald's perspective is complicated by a personal involvement with his heroes' struggles, and an inability to decide whether their ambitions are glorious and admirable or futile and destructive. In short, the differences between Lardner's and Fitzgerald's treatment of the theme of the social adventurer are emphatic. Still, it is essentially the same drama that engages the two authors. Again and again, both trace the pattern of the failure of social aspiration, a pattern that parallels what was happening all around them in the life of the period.

In one of his familiar essays Fitzgerald claimed that professional writers have only two or three stories to tell, which they repeat in different disguises "as long as people will listen." One of the stories Fitzgerald relied on—perhaps more than any of the others—is basically the same story the reader encounters in the pages of Ring Lardner. With neither author, however, is the story a simple one.

It was along last January when I and the Wife was both hit by the society bacillus [says the hero of "Gullible's Travels"]. You remember me tellin' you about us and the Hatches goin' to *Carmen* and then me takin' my Missus and her sister, Bess, and four of one suit named Bishop to see *The Three Kings?* Well, I'll own up that I enjoyed wearin' the soup and fish and minglin' amongst the high polloi and pretendin' we really was somebody. And I know

> my wife enjoyed it, too, though they was nothin' said
> between us at the time.
>
> The next stage was where our friends wasn't quite good
> enough for us no more. . . .
>
> We quit attendin' pitcher shows because the rest o' the
> audience wasn't the kind o' people you'd care to mix
> with. . . .
>
> Then we took to readin' the society news at breakfast. . . .

Here, in unblushing directness, is a definitive statement
of the situation that appealed so strongly to Lardner's imagination. But it represents only the first step in a truly ambitious undertaking. The "wise boob" hero and his Missus
can do more than read the society news at breakfast: they
have the financial means to equip themselves with two
train tickets, new wardrobes, and accommodations at a
good resort hotel. These are, at first glance, the only requirements for easy access to the world of the leisure class.

> We'd be staying under the same roof with the Vanderbilts
> and Goulds, and eatin' at the same table, and probably,
> before we was there a week, callin' 'em Steve and Gus. . . .
> And all Chicago society was down there, and when we met
> 'em we'd know 'em for life and have some real friends
> amongst 'em when we got back home.

The ascent to the halls of Privilege, in actuality, is not
this simple, as Lardner's innocents discover. The closest
approach to the desired acceptance comes at the end of
the story, when the narrator and his wife, having been
ignored by everyone save waiters and bus boys, encounter
a genuine representative of the aristocracy:

> "It's Mrs. Potter," [the Missus] says; "*the* Mrs. Potter from
> Chicago!"
>
> "Oh!" I says, puttin' all the excitement I could into my
> voice.
>
> And I was just startin' back into the room when I seen

Mrs. Potter stop and turn around and come to'rd us. She stopped again maybe twenty feet from where the Missus was standin'.

"Are you on this floor?" she says.

The Missus shook like a leaf.

"Yes," says she, so low you couldn't hardly hear her.

"Please see that they's some towels put in 559," says *the* Mrs. Potter from Chicago.

This saga of the social climber is, of course, caricature; yet it is remarkable how many stories and novels produced during the decade were to parallel its general outline. And for Lardner himself there were other, more disturbing areas of the subject to be explored. As in "Gullible's Travels," so in a number of other stories he portrays the *nouveaux riches* as harboring an intense but frustrated desire for ease and gracious living, which they assume will automatically attend their entry into upper economic strata. The consequences of this false assumption are sometimes disastrous.

"The Love Nest," for example, is clearly a variation on Lardner's theme of the disappointed parvenu. But Celia Gregg's disappointment is not presented in the comic spirit of "Gullible's Travels." It is savage, resentful, and profoundly bitter. She has married for money, Celia explains to the reporter who comes to do a feature story on the domestic life of the "great man" (Celia's husband); but her anticipated contentment has failed to materialize:

> "You're dumb, Barker! You may be sober, but you're dumb! Did you fall for all that apple sauce about the happy home and the contented wife? Listen, Barker—I'd give anything in the world to be out of this mess. I'd give anything to never see him again."
>
> "Don't you love him any more? Doesn't he love you? Or what?"
>
> "Love! I never did love him! I didn't know what love was! And all his love is for himself!"

"How did you happen to get married?"

"I was a kid; that's the answer. A kid and ambitious. See? He was a director then and he got stuck on me and I thought he'd make me a star. See, Barker? I married him to get myself a chance. And now look at me!"

"I'd say you were fairly well off."

"Well off, am I? I'd change places with the scum of the earth just to be free! See, Barker? And I could have been a star without any help if I'd only realized it. I had the looks and I had the talent. I've got it yet. I could be a Swanson and get myself a marquis; maybe a prince! And look what I did get! A self-satisfied, self-centered ——! I thought he'd *make* me! See, Barker? Well, he's made me all right; he's made me a chronic mother and it's a wonder I've got any looks left.

"I fought at first. I told him marriage didn't mean giving up my art, my life work. But it was no use. He wanted a beautiful wife and beautiful children for his beautiful home. Just to show us off. See? I'm part of his chattels. See, Barker? I'm just like his big diamond or his cars or his horses."

And there are Ella and Kate, of "The Big Town," whose father dies of grief when the war ends and cuts short his unscrupulous profiteering. He leaves his daughters two hundred thousand dollars, and the heiresses immediately "run over to Chi and buy all the party dresses that was vacant. Then they come back to South Bend, and wished somebody would give a party." South Bend, of course, can no longer satisfy their craving for Life, nor can it provide a rich husband for Sister Kate. The family migrates to New York, there to encounter a varied assortment of crooks, cheats, and frauds—a cross section of Lardner's middle-class America. At one point in their adventures, Ella and Kate have placed a bet of twelve hundred dollars on a horse named Only One, a wager strongly urged by the horse's owner. Lardner memorably records their reaction to the news Only One has lost the race:

> The gals sunk down in their chairs. Ella was blubbering and Kate was white as a ghost.
> "I can't understand it!" [the owner] says. "I don't know what happened!"
> "You don't!" hollered Kate. "I'll tell you what happened. You stole our money! Twelve hundred dollars! You cheat!"

These characters and many others who participate in the grim Lardner comedy all fall victim sooner or later to essentially the same assumption. They have recently acquired great sums of money, and consequently they claim a right to the kind of life they naively associate with wealth. Whatever it is they seek—luxury, fame, social distinction, or culture (see the story "Carmen")—Lardner's final judgment of these would-be gentlemen and women is unequivocal: all suffer some fundamental defect of character that disqualifies them from enjoying their riches. Their newly acquired wealth only intensifies their unaristocratic condition.

But Lardner's final irony is contained in his portrayal of the "aristocrats" who very infrequently appear in his fiction. Lady Perkins, the self-styled English noblewoman of "The Big Town," is the most unforgettable representative of this class: she turns out to be as fiercely avaricious and as blatantly crude as the mass of aspirers who seek to win her favor.[7] "Contract," Lardner's miniature of manners at the card table, illustrates the same point. Shelton, the hero, has recently acquired money and position: "Shelton's magazine had advanced him to a position as associate editor and he was able, with the assistance of a benignant bond and

---

[7] *The* Mrs. Potter of "Gullible's Travels" is another of the "aristocrats" Lardner satirizes. An interesting parallel may be found in Sinclair Lewis's treatment of Sir Gerald Doak, the Babbitty English nobleman in *Babbitt*.

mortgage company, to move into a house in Linden." Shelton
and his wife are soon involved in a round of bridge parties
with other *nouveaux riches* suburbanites who exasperate
them with their jocose vulgarity and transparent affecta-
tions, and continually criticize their inexpert attempts to
play contract bridge. Shelton avenges himself one night by
correcting everyone's table manners and bad grammar. But
when the Sheltons, having deserted the circle of boors,
manage an invitation to play cards at "the palatial home of
E. M. Pardee, one of the real aristocrats of Linden," they
encounter the same rudeness from which they have fled,
only a week earlier, in disgust:

> After dinner, Mrs. Pardee asked the Sheltons whether
> they played contract, and they said they did. The Pardees,
> not wishing to impoverish the young immigrants, refused
> to play "families." They insisted on cutting and Shelton cut
> Mrs. Pardee.
> "Oh, Mr. Shevlin," she said at the end of the first hand,
> "why *didn't* you lead me a club? You must watch the dis-
> cards!"

The implication of these examples is clear: the ambition
of the parvenu is hopelessly unattainable. What the predatory social climber is pursuing does not exist, except as an
ideal in his own pathetic imaginings.

The typical Fitzgerald hero bears a remarkable resemblance to Lardner's aggressive social climber. He too has
been infected by the "society bacillus" that beset the humorist's naive parvenu. The malignancy is more subtle,
sublimating social ambition into nice distinctions, as in the
case of Dexter Green in "Winter Dreams": "He wanted not
association with glittering things and glittering people—he
wanted the glittering things themselves." Nevertheless,

Dexter Green wants what virtually all Fitzgerald's heroes want: social superiority, refinement, magnificence. In Lardner's phrase, Fitzgerald's sad young men want acceptance "amongst the high polloi."

There are, however, significant differences in Fitzgerald's conception of the subject. The hero of the Fitzgerald romance does not "discover" social possibilities suddenly, as do Lardner's enterprising social climbers. Instead, he awakens to them early—usually in childhood—and thereafter earnestly pursues a course upward toward fulfillment of the American Dream of status and "success."

It is this deeply felt, almost compulsive ambition that motivates Dexter Green to "pass up a business course at the State University—his father, prospering now, would have paid his way—for the precarious advantage of attending an older and more famous university in the East. . . ." Once out of college, Green amasses quick wealth in the laundry business; but neither higher education nor riches can assure the fulfillment of the hero's "dream." For the heroine remains skeptical of Dexter's qualifications as a member of her class. Judy Jones, the beautiful debutante of "Winter Dreams," thinks him suitable for a brief love affair which "endured just one month." But she will not seriously consider marriage to Dexter Green; and at last he abandons his dream of attaining this country-club chimera, the exciting and elusive figure on the moonlit veranda who, mysteriously, is not for him: "he did not possess in himself the power to move fundamentally or to hold Judy Jones. . . . He loved her, and he would love her until the day he was too old for loving—but he could not have her."

The story of Dexter Green and Judy Jones crystallizes one of Fitzgerald's most essential parables, one that was admirably suited to the tone and tempo of the nineteen-twenties. Perhaps much of his own generation's fascination with Fitzgerald may be attributed to his repeated emphasis on the two major themes that appear uniquely intermingled in "Winter Dreams"—social aspiration and romantic love.

"Winter Dreams" is clearly a preparation for *The Great Gatsby;* the short story sounds certain themes which Fitzgerald orchestrates more fully in the novel. Like Dexter Green, the hero of *The Great Gatsby* has his "dreams"— which emerge as brilliant and limitless fantasies beckoning him on to an extravagant extreme of American success. Like Dexter Green, Gatsby covets The Girl, who in his eyes represents a way of life almost inconceivably glamorous, exciting, and desirable. At first an outsider at the gates of her world, the hero can gain admission only by the boldness of a timely opportunism:

> But he knew that he was in Daisy's house by a colossal accident. However glorious might be his future as Jay Gatsby, he was at present a penniless young man without a past, and at any moment the invisible cloak of his uniform might slip from his shoulders. So he made the most of his time. He took what he could get, ravenously and unscrupulously—eventually he took Daisy one still October night, took her because he had no real right to touch her hand.
>
> He might have despised himself, for he had certainly taken her under false pretenses. I don't mean that he had traded on his phantom millions, but he had deliberately given Daisy a sense of security; he let her believe that he was a person from much the same strata as herself—that he was fully able to take care of her. As a matter of fact, he had no such facilities—he had no comfortable family standing behind him, and he was liable at the whim of an impersonal government to be blown anywhere about the world.

Later, Gatsby indulges in an elaborate, costly project which includes the purchase of a feudal mansion on Long

Island, "full of interesting people . . . celebrated people," a wardrobe of silver shirts and golden ties, a continuous series of gaudy parties, and a romantic "background" made to order from bits and scraps of the hero's past. All this, and more, Gatsby contrives as part of the same self-improvement program thought *de rigueur* by Dexter Green and Lardner's innocents, who yearn for culture and social distinction. At times, in fact, Fitzgerald abandons the fantasies of his glamorous protagonist to strike the same note of ruthless satire that one encounters in Lardner. Myrtle Wilson, Tom Buchanan's vulgar mistress, exchanges confidences with one of her pretentious friends:

> "I almost made a mistake, too," [Mrs. McKee] declared vigorously. "I almost married a little kike who'd been after me for years. I knew he was below me. Everybody kept saying to me: 'Lucille, that man's 'way below you!' But if I hadn't met Chester, he'd of got me sure."
>
> "Yes, but listen," said Myrtle Wilson, nodding her head up and down, "at least you didn't marry him."
>
> "I know I didn't."
>
> "Well, I married him," said Myrtle ambiguously. "And that's the difference between your case and mine."
>
> "Why did you, Myrtle?" demanded Catherine. "Nobody forced you to."
>
> Myrtle considered.
>
> "I married him because I thought he was a gentleman," she said finally. "I thought he knew something about breeding, but he wasn't fit to lick my shoe."

Celia Gregg, the heroine of Lardner's "Love Nest," had similar great expectations: "I could be a Swanson and get myself a marquis; maybe a prince!"

These pretensions and yearnings, both in Lardner and Fitzgerald, end in frustration: Celia Gregg's only comfort is furtive alcoholism; Myrtle Wilson's struggles end in death; and Gatsby's extravagances are unavailing. Daisy Fay, the enchantress with money in her voice, remains "high in a white palace the king's daughter, the golden girl. . . ." She is beyond Gatsby's reach.

The fate of the Fitzgerald hero almost invariably follows this pattern of aspiration and failure. To be sure, certain details of each individual history are unique: Amory Blaine suffers from a bad case of poverty; Gatsby does not "belong" in Daisy's world; and Dexter Green's social deficiencies qualify him merely to feed Judy Jones's appetite for adoration. Gordon Sterrett, the protagonist of "May Day," finds life intolerable because he cannot locate himself socially. Sterrett doesn't have the money to be accepted into the world of Philip Dean, his former classmate; and he lacks the ability to become a self-made Alger hero. Trapped into a marriage with a girl his friends consider vulgar, he commits suicide. Andy, the narrator of "The Last of the Belles," cannot hope to hold the affections of Allie Calhoun as long as he continues to see through her social pretensions; Dick Diver, having once accepted a dependent position as Nicole Warren's salaried caretaker, cannot claim equality in her milieu.

In addition, Fitzgerald's protagonists suffer different kinds and degrees of distress, ranging from sophomoric self-pity to utter and inescapable devastation. Amory emerges with crushed emotions and bittersweet memories; Dexter Green loses what he has cherished most highly—the optimistic illusions of his youth; Gatsby loses his life; and Dick Diver sacrifices his vitality and ambition. But the reader should not underestimate the equally important uniformity that shapes the contour of these histories. For it is clear that all these sad young men are engaged in the same struggle; Fitzgerald's foremost tale of the Jazz Age was based on an assumption that was shared by his real-life contemporaries: it is possible to be anything one dreams of being, to become a part of any milieu one chooses as desirable. That is the dream. But the reality, at least as Fitzgerald presents it in his serious fiction, is disappointment.

The forces that defeat Fitzgerald's heroes are far more complicated and more seriously considered than those that confront Lardner's social climbers. Lardner's middle-class aspirers fail because of social ineptness and stupidity (ironically shared by parvenu and "aristocrat" alike). Fitzgerald's social drama implies a fundamental incompatibility between the classes: he consistently portrays the members of the American "aristocracy" as a class apart, insulated from intrusion by outsiders. "Let me tell you," Fitzgerald says in one of his most celebrated pronouncements, "about the very rich":

> They are different from you and me. They possess and enjoy early, and it does something to them, makes them soft where we are hard, and cynical where we are trustful, in a way that, unless you were born rich, it is very difficult to understand. They think, deep in their hearts, that they are better than we are because we had to discover the compensations and refuges of life for ourselves. Even when they enter deep into our world or sink below us, they still think that they are better than we are. They are different.

Fitzgerald goes on, in the story that follows this brief introduction, to display some evidences of this difference and its inherent consequences. The Rich Boy, Anson Hunter, unwittingly permits a cold superiority to dominate his actions; his fastidious and egotistical nature will not allow him to forgive; it will not allow him to love. It renders him an outcast from life's feast.

But "The Rich Boy" illustrates only one form the difference may take. Daisy and Tom Buchanan, of *The Great Gatsby*, are different by virtue of an ingrained ethical "carelessness":

> They were careless people, Tom and Daisy—they smashed up things and creatures and then retreated back into their money or their vast carelessness, or whatever it was that kept them together, and let other people clean up the mess they had made. . . .

And Baby Warren and Nicole Diver (after she has regained her sanity) are different by virtue of their assumption that all things, including people, are available to serve their needs.

Thus the cycle of action represented in Fitzgerald's mature works leads from the *naif's* eager courtship of the aristocracy, to the failure of his suit and the revelation that he has wooed an unworthy and faithless mistress. Lardner's interest in the same cycle of action is evident, though he treats his heroes' ambitions and defeats less gravely. Yet in both authors, there is a repeated and disillusioned emphasis on the futility of the would-be gentleman's dream.

In certain areas, then—particularly in their treatments of the theme of the social adventurer—Lardner and Fitzgerald seem to display a number of similar attitudes: they fashion their stories from similar materials; they seem in accord in their conclusions. Yet there is an underlying difference in their interpretations of this pattern in American experience. One cannot escape the impression, in reading Fitzgerald, that his melancholy and romantic heroes are re-enacting the author's own pilgrimage to the shrine of wealth, success, and the beautiful heroine—that however critical Fitzgerald may be of the corruption, superiority, and inhumanity of the American rich, parts of his fiction represent a subtle tribute to his own yearning to be one of them. In "The Crack-Up"

Fitzgerald spoke of how he had cherished "an abiding distrust, an animosity, toward the leisure class"; but later in the same series of essays he admitted that his depressed condition was the result of his having become identified "with the objects of my horror or compassion." Apparently Fitzgerald suffered from a division of sympathies whenever he undertook to delineate his most essential theme.

Ring Lardner suffered no such conflict in his attitudes toward American society, nor do his works reveal the haunting ambiguities that oppressed Fitzgerald's sensibility. Throughout Lardner's fiction runs the implication that the author feels superior in intelligence and breeding to the society his heroes and heroines want so desperately to crash. To Fitzgerald's confident assertion that "the very rich are different from you and me," Lardner might have replied: "No, there is no difference." Or perhaps: "Yes, if anything they are a bit cruder." Lardner, like Mencken, looked upon the pretensions of the middle class as a joke—sometimes ugly, sometimes merely amusing or pathetic in its futility. To Fitzgerald the dream was no joke, but a hope and something of a lifelong passion.

Under Lardner's influence, however, Fitzgerald's unfavorable impressions of the American rich emerged in greater clarity than ever before. That influence finds expression within the complicated framework of *The Great Gatsby*.

III

Fitzgerald's interest in sports is well known, and has been documented by his biographers and critics. During his days at prep school, and later at Princeton, one of Fitzgerald's ambitions was to be a football hero; his failure on the field seemed to be a source of deep regret, as well as self-accusation, in the years that followed. It is recorded that as late as twenty years after his graduation the novelist frequently made long-distance telephone calls to the Princeton football coach to offer advice and occasional criticism of the team's performance. This interest in football is reflected in parts of *This Side of Paradise* and in several short stories and informal essays Fitzgerald wrote during different periods of his career. There are also a few scattered and insignificant references to golfing in some of the stories written in the twenties. But it was not until *The Great Gatsby* that Fitzgerald introduced the game of baseball into his fiction.

Lardner, of course, was closely associated with this sport. For many years he traveled with baseball teams and acted as sports reporter for various metropolitan newspapers; and he is perhaps best remembered as an author for his vernacular studies of ballplayers and their sometimes comic, sometimes grotesque eccentricities. It is highly probable that the subject of baseball frequently came up during the period of Fitzgerald's stay in Great Neck, when in his own words he and Lardner "tucked a lot under their belts in many weathers, and spent many words on many men and things." But more relevant to the composition of *The Great Gatsby* is the particular attitude toward American sports Lardner had evolved by the time of his association with Fitzgerald. Lardner had suffered disillusion with athletics in general and baseball in particular, as is apparent in works such as "Champion" (1916), "You Know Me, Al" (1914), his syndicated column (1919-27), and a great many short stories about ballplaying cranks, troublemakers, and neurotics. A glance at Lardner's contribution to the symposium *Civilization in the United States*—published the same year Fitzgerald arrived in Great Neck—discloses strong evidence of this dissatisfaction: "In blissful asininity, we may feast our eyes on the swarthy Champion of swat, shouting now and then in an excess of anile idolatry, 'Come on, you Babe. Come

on, you Baby Doll!' " Even more to the point is the fact that
Lardner's disenchantment was simultaneously confirmed and
nourished by the World Series of 1919, a focal point in
sports history to which he repeatedly alluded in later years.

When, in 1920, it was made public that members of the
Chicago White Sox team had been bribed, Lardner commented sardonically: "[The Series] was won by the Cincin-
nati Reds greatly to their surprise." But Lardner's feelings
about the scandal went deeper than the offhand tone of
this comment might suggest. "For Ring," Donald Elder tells
us, "baseball was not the same after 1919. . . . In spite of
his knowing that ball players were as corruptible as anyone
else, the whole episode was bitterly shocking and too close
to him to be passed off philosophically." [8] The World Series
of 1919 helped deepen Lardner's cynical attitude toward
commercialized sports and toward the widespread corruption that was to characterize so much of the public life of
the nineteen-twenties. It probably contributed, too, to the
impression Fitzgerald received of Lardner as a "disillusioned
idealist."

It is this same World Series, used in a context of similar
disillusion, that Fitzgerald incorporated into the novel he
wrote almost immediately after he had enjoyed his close
companionship with Ring Lardner. Fitzgerald, of course,
must have heard of the Black Sox scandal before that time;
anyone interested in sports would have had some knowledge
of that highly publicized and much discussed event. But
the circumstances outlined above—and the function of the
World Series episode in *The Great Gatsby*—strongly suggest
Lardner's direct influence on this portion of Fitzgerald's
novel.

It is, furthermore, no trivial or incidental role that the
World Series allusions play in *Gatsby*. They occupy a

[8] *Ring Lardner* (New York, 1956), pp. 162-163.

prominent position in Nick Carraway's developing sense of "the fundamental decencies":

> "Fixed the World's Series?" I repeated.
> The idea staggered me. I remembered, of course, that the World's Series had been fixed in 1919, but if I had thought of it at all I would have thought of it as a thing that merely *happened,* the end of some inevitable chain. It never occurred to me that one man could start to play with the faith of fifty million people. . . .

Nick's reaction here is only one element in a subtle pattern woven throughout his entire experience in the book. Wolfsheim's act of tampering with the faith of fifty million people is related to Daisy's betrayal of Gatsby, to Tom Buchanan's marital infidelity, to Nick's own position in regard to the deceit, treachery, and bad faith practiced by the major characters of the novel. It is related to the period of Nick's employment at the "Probity Trust," during which time he hangs suspended between awareness of good and evil, and its negation. Furthermore, as Gatsby's business partner, Wolfsheim is linked to the hero's illegally acquired riches, an association that helps us to understand Gatsby's desperate determination to impress Daisy, at whatever cost. In Fitzgerald's hands, the World Series image attains minor but important symbolic significance in *The Great Gatsby.* If Lardner provided the original inspiration, the full realization of its potential value must be credited to Fitzgerald's imaginative adaptation.

This process of artistic elaboration is even more apparent in another instance of Fitzgerald's debt to Lardner. The inspiration in this case stems from Lardner's story "A Caddy's Diary," originally published in 1922 in the *Saturday Evening Post* and later reprinted in *How To Write Short Stories* (1925). Since Fitzgerald supervised the preparation of this volume, it is certain that he was acquainted with the curiously memorable fable of country-club golfers it contained. Internal evidence in *The Great Gatsby* confirms Fitzgerald's intimate knowledge of the story.

"A Caddy's Diary" takes the form of a day-to-day record kept by a boy named Dick, "16 of age . . . and a caddy at the Pleasant View Golf Club." The action in the story is seen through the eyes of Lardner's adolescent narrator, who, like Nick Carraway in *The Great Gatsby*, plays an apparently minor role in the main drama. But Dick and Nick Carraway both occupy ambiguous positions in their relation to the characters around them. Their presence may be taken merely as an artistic stratagem to attain verisimilitude; or they may be seen as protagonists in their own right, the central intelligence and major figure in the world each inhabits. The parallel extends even further: both Dick and Carraway come into close contact with a variety of cheats, liars, amoral and immoral characters of all sorts, representatives of what Carraway alludes to as the "rotten crowd" around Gatsby, the "foul dust that floated in the wake of his dreams"; both narrators are frequently in danger of being drawn into the general wickedness and moral laxity; both contribute, at one time or another, to that wickedness; and finally both develop a keener sense of moral awareness as they encounter a wider diversity of disenchanting experience.[9]

Lardner has created his narrator with skill and insight; and the story Caddy Dick tells has a disturbing and intense seriousness that gives it more than casual significance. But Nick Carraway's world is larger; his responses to experience

[9] Other critics, notably James E. Miller, have advanced the idea that Fitzgerald's inspiration for Nick Carraway was the Marlow stories of Joseph Conrad. The Lardner source now seems to me to be the more likely possibility.

are more complicated; his sensibility is more mature; and the actions which he records are of greater consequence than those which take place at Lardner's country club. Fitzgerald elaborated upon his source, investing it with increased scope and complexity. Other elements Fitzgerald derived from "A Caddy's Diary" illustrate equally well the same process of artistic transmutation.

"A Caddy's Diary" exposes the pettiness and meanness—and the confused moral standards—of a modern upper-middle-class community. Most of the members of the Pleasant View Golf Club bribe or coerce their caddies, cheat their fellow players, and lie about their scores whenever the opportunity presents itself. Some of the players observe the letter of the golfing laws, but not their spirit; they are masters in the art of how to win without actually cheating. The only characters in the story who play an honest game are Charles Crane, who turns out to be a thief; and Jack Andrews, the club pro, who earns "a small steady income" by playing less than his best game with one of the club members he knows he can beat. Joe Bean, one of the caddies, explains why these two men never lie about their scores:

> Players like Crane and Andrews that goes around in 80 or better can't cheat on their score because they make most of the holes in around 4 strokes and the 4 strokes includes their tee shot and a couple of putts which everybody is right there to watch them when they make them and count them right along with them . . . that is one of the penaltys for being a good player, you can't cheat.

Obviously both Crane and Andrews—along with most of the other club members—are hypocrites. In addition, one of the women members is given to outbursts of obscene language, and all the rest are grasping mercenaries who readily sacrifice the rules of the game to a grand avarice for petty rewards. Mrs. Thomas, realizing that she cannot possibly win the match with Miss Rennie, insists upon searching for a lost ball until the game has to be called off on account of darkness; thereby she avoids paying Miss Rennie the twenty-five-cent wager agreed upon. Mr. Thomas and Mr. Dunham exchange vicious insults when they are "off" in their games. One of the older members smashes his four wood clubs against a tree in a fit of temper. Mr. Thomas, who thinks "golf is wrong on the sabbath," misrepresents his score in order to win the tournament prize of nine golf balls. And the caddies, hoping to earn large tips, gladly assist in the players' deceptions. Caddy Dick willingly cheats for a pretty woman player in order to earn the reward of her smile.

When at the end of the story Charles Crane absconds with his secretary and eight thousand dollars stolen from the bank where he is employed, the members of the Pleasant View Golf Club pounce upon this act of outright dishonesty to sermonize upon their own righteousness. Only Dick and Joe Bean (who all along has commented cynically and shrewdly upon the players' conduct) ponder the true issues raised by Crane's act:

Well I said it seems to me like these people have got a lot of nerve to pan Mr Crane and call him a sucker for doing what he done, it seems to me like $8000 and a swell dame is a pretty fair reward compared with what some of these other people sells their soul for, and I would like to tell them about it.

Well said Joe go ahead and tell them but maybe they will tell you something right back.

What will they tell me?

Well said Joe they might tell you this, that when Mr Thomas asks you how many shots he has had and you say 4

when you know he has had 5, why you are selling your soul
for a $1.00 tip. And when you move Mrs Doanes ball out
of a rut and give it a good lie, what are you selling your
soul for? Just a smile.

Fitzgerald borrowed from "A Caddy's Diary" when he
came to create the moral atmosphere of *The Great Gatsby;*
but once again, he expanded and subtilized the original. In
addition to exploring an entire scale of ethical values—from
Tom Buchanan's amoral attitudes to Gatsby's ethical compromises and Nick Carraway's persistent and sometimes
puzzled moral judgments—Fitzgerald considers the complicated subject of differing varieties of falsehood; the author's
treatment of this theme suggests the manner of a technician
weighing assertions on a delicate instrument designed to
calculate the falseness of a lie. When Tom Buchanan directs
Myrtle Wilson's husband to Gatsby's house, he is probably
lying to shield Daisy from having to admit her responsibility
for Myrtle's death. Later, he justifies this act to Nick
Carraway by a neat bit of sophistry (the italics are mine):

> "I told him the truth," he said. "He came to the door while
> we were getting ready to leave, and when I sent down word
> that we weren't in he tried to force his way upstairs. He
> was crazy enough to kill me if I hadn't told him *who owned
> the car.*"

Of course, Gatsby does own the car, but it was Daisy who
struck down and killed Myrtle Wilson. On the other hand,
if Tom believes what he says later in the same passage—"He
ran over Myrtle like you'd run over a dog and never even
stopped the car"—then Daisy is the liar who brings about
the injustice of Gatsby's death. The text of the novel does not
provide a conclusive answer to the question of Buchanan's
veracity in this crucial matter (though Fitzgerald has him
tell several lies earlier); rather, Fitzgerald encourages the

reader to explore further the "relative-falsehood" theme that is interwoven throughout the fabric of the book.

Gatsby, to cite another example, is uncompromisingly dedicated to the attainment of love, prosperity, and status. He is committed, as Lionel Trilling has remarked of Fitzgerald, to an ideal of self. But Gatsby compromises his ethics drastically in his manner of money-getting, as his association with Meyer Wolfsheim attests. Opposed to Tom Buchanan's deliberate and outright lies is Gatsby's concoction of a personal "history" composed of half-truths. Myrtle Wilson's life with her husband is a lie, as is Tom's with Daisy, and Daisy's with Tom, once she re-encounters Gatsby on Long Island. It is a lie, in fact, that leads to the murder of Gatsby. Jordan Baker lies repeatedly, and Nick Carraway compromises with truth in the matter of his self-estimate early in the novel: "Everyone suspects himself of at least one of the cardinal virtues, and this is mine: I am one of the few honest people I have ever known." This compromise with truth is paralleled by Nick's ethical compromises occurring throughout the central section of the book, when (to mention only a few instances) he plays panderer for Jay Gatsby and he becomes intimate with the "incurably dishonest" Miss Jordan Baker. Fitzgerald's purpose in detailing this relativity of truth and falsehood—and its accompanying moral confusion—is partially clarified by Nick's statement to Jordan at the end of the novel:

> "I thought you were rather an honest, straightforward person [Jordan says to Nick]. I thought it was your secret pride."
> "I'm thirty," I said. "I'm five years too old to lie to myself and call it honor."

Having begun with a complacent confidence in his own honor ("I am one of the few. . . ."), Nick profits from his exposure to experience by losing his illusions about himself.

The theme of relative truth and morality contributes strongly to our understanding of the world of experience as Fitzgerald presents it in *The Great Gatsby*, a world inhabited by Gatsby, the Buchanans, Myrtle and George Wilson, and—for a time—Nick Carraway. It is insubstantial, elusive as a dream, full of "somewhat truthful" assertions, fatal and near-fatal self-delusions, and nebulous treacheries. Long Island is Fitzgerald's "unreal city," as London was T. S. Eliot's, as the Pleasant View Golf Club was Ring Lardner's. These settings are characterized by an absence of fixed ethical standards, by a lack of any foundation in truth or morality. When Nick says good-by to Jordan Baker, he is renouncing the world in which she lives. When he starts for home, he is entering reality.

It is highly probable that Fitzgerald was inspired to the use of this intricate "relative truth and morality" theme by "A Caddy's Diary"; it is all but certain that he took at least one of its components from that source. Prominent among the characters in Lardner's story is the attractive Mrs. Doane, who during a particular golf match has wagered fifty dollars against a party dress owned by her opponent. At one point when she is unobserved, Mrs. Doane asks Dick to move the ball from a bad lie:

> Do I have to play it from there she said.
>
> I guess you do was my reply.
>
> Why Dick have you went back on me she said and give me one of her looks.
>
> Well I looked to see if the others was looking and then I kind of give the ball a shove with my toe and it come out of the groove and laid where she could get a swipe at it. This was the 16th hole and Mrs Doane win it by 11 strokes to 10 and that made her 2 up and 2 to go. Miss Rennie win the 17th but they both took a 10 for the 18th and that give Mrs Doane the match.

Compare this episode with Nick Carraway's sudden recollection:

> When we were out on a house-party together up in Warwick, [Jordan] left a borrowed car out in the rain with the top down, and then lied about it—and suddenly I remembered the story about her that had eluded me that night at Daisy's. At her first big golf tournament there was a row that nearly reached the newspapers—a suggestion that she had moved her ball from a bad lie in the semi-final round. The thing approached the proportions of a scandal—then died away. A caddy retracted his statement, and the only other witness admitted that he might have been mistaken.

Mrs. Doane has stepped from the green at the Pleasant View Golf Club into the pages of *The Great Gatsby* to become Jordan Baker, one of the most memorable of Fitzgerald's fictional characters.

The metamorphosis of Mrs. Doane into Jordan Baker is another illustration of the manner in which a superior artist brings to fulfillment the latent value of material derived from a literary source. As stressed throughout this section, Lardner supplied his fellow author with relatively bare, unelaborated images; Fitzgerald's own artistry is finally responsible for the development of these basic themes, characters, and situations in *The Great Gatsby*.

Thus the peculiar alchemy of literary influence, when two such apparently dissimilar works as "A Caddy's Diary" and *The Great Gatsby* under close scrutiny reveal the deepest of affinities and show one writer's mark upon the imagination of another. Aside from bringing to light a long neglected source of inspiration for Fitzgerald's most highly regarded work of fiction, the extended comparison of these two writers should also provide a new perspective—a point of reference from which we may study one artist as he relates to one of his contemporaries, and both as they relate to their age.

Thus, too, a welcome opportunity to represent Ring Lardner at some length in his own voice—by no means an incidental part of my intention in this chapter. Lardner deserves more than incidental study. At his best he performed brilliantly in a demanding and, for us, highly instructive role—as a miniaturist depicting the vices and follies of an unhealthy society. Like the deft and merciless engravers of eighteenth-century England, Lardner evoked vivid images that serve as indictments of our moral compromises and hypocrisies. From Lardner, the Hogarth of our literature, Fitzgerald learned the means to bring into sharp focus his own feelings about the Tom and Daisy Buchanans in American society and their "vast carelessness" in human relations.

Fitzgerald's canvas is broader than Lardner's, and he has color—subtle, delicate, sometimes dazzling in its display of showy brightness, always appealing, suggestive of new meanings and fresh discoveries. Yet color is not enough. Fitzgerald's early novels, as his commentators have frequently noted, lack the detachment necessary to transmute his intensely felt personal impressions into mature art. With *The Great Gatsby*, Fitzgerald achieved that detachment—the product, no doubt, of much diligent and independent disciplining of his talent. But the penetrating criticism of American mores in *Gatsby* may also be attributed, in part, to Fitzgerald's intimate association with Ring Lardner. Lardner and his unique works of fiction left an indelible impression on the young novelist from the Midwest, who, like Gatsby, came East to test the wonders of sophisticated America.

CHAPTER V

Ernest Hemingway

> "I hear distant thunder about Ernest. . . ."
> —FITZGERALD TO GERALD MURPHY

Writers, said Ernest Hemingway in *Green Hills of Africa,*
should work alone. Hemingway was thinking of the dangers
of cliquish inbreeding, the vitiating consequences of depend-
ing too exclusively on the stimulation provided by other
writers. "They should see each other only after their work
is done, and not too often then," the novelist added. "Otherwise they become like writers in New York. All angleworms
in a bottle, trying to derive knowledge and nourishment
from their own contact and from the bottle. Sometimes
the bottle is shaped art, sometimes economics, sometimes
economic-religion. But once they are in the bottle they stay
there. They are lonesome outside the bottle."

Perhaps it was the fear of being trapped inside some such
"bottle" that prompted Scott Fitzgerald to leave New York
hastily for Europe in the spring of 1924. Certainly the
routine of wild parties, extravagant spending, and the by

now familiar faces of New York "literary friends" had something to do with Fitzgerald's decision to seek change—and perhaps refreshment for the imagination—on foreign shores. "We were going to the Old World," the author wrote later, "to find a new rhythm for our lives, with a true conviction that we had left our old selves behind forever. . . ."

Whatever his motives for leaving the United States, it is certain that during his travels abroad Fitzgerald felt drawn to the company of numerous expatriate American and native British authors; he looked up Compton Mackenzie, who had strongly influenced *This Side of Paradise*, and T. S. Eliot—as on a trip a few years earlier he had looked up John Galsworthy and James Joyce. On this second sojourn, which was to last more than two years, Fitzgerald also attended a number of parties in Paris and on the Riviera where he met (or renewed his acquaintance with) Alexander Woollcott, Archibald MacLeish, John Dos Passos, and Donald Ogden Stewart. During this period he also spent an afternoon with Edith Wharton; and he met Ezra Pound and the group that circulated around Gertrude Stein. Fitzgerald entered into this round of social activity with enthusiasm; but he was most impressed by Ernest Hemingway, whose name begins to appear with increasing frequency in 1925 in Fitzgerald's letters to friends at home. To Mencken he wrote that he had met the circle of American writers in Paris, and they were mostly "junk-dealers." The exception, Fitzgerald added, was a fellow named Hemingway, who was doing more thinking and working than the young writers back home. To Edmund Wilson, Fitzgerald announced that he had met Hemingway, who had promised to take him to see Gertrude Stein. A few months later Fitzgerald wrote to John Peale Bishop, listing rather proudly the distinguished company he had been keeping that summer at Antibes and closing with the information that "the Hemingways" were coming to dinner.

Fitzgerald's first encounter with Hemingway dates from the year preceding these references. He had seen some of Hemingway's work in 1924 and had written to Maxwell Perkins: "This is to tell you about a young writer named Ernest Hemingway, who lives in Paris . . . writes for the *transatlantic review,* and has a brilliant future. I'd look him up right away. He's the real thing." Hemingway had already signed a contract with Boni and Liveright; but soon afterwards Liveright editors rejected *Torrents of Spring* (it parodied their most valuable author, Sherwood Anderson); and Hemingway was again at liberty to choose a publisher, several of whom were now soliciting his work. Hemingway's decision to sign with Maxwell Perkins at Scribner's was strongly influenced by Fitzgerald's repeated recommendations. Fitzgerald's part in this transaction reflects his interest in furthering Hemingway's career; it is one episode in the campaign Fitzgerald undertook to help his new friend gain recognition during the period 1924-1926. These years formed the early stages of what was to develop into a relationship that continued, amid emotional depths and unexpected turns, until Fitzgerald's death in 1940.

Perhaps the most revealing record of Fitzgerald's attitude toward Hemingway during this period is found in Glenway Wescott's memorial essay, "The Moral of Scott Fitzgerald," written in 1941:

> Hemingway had published some short stories in the dinky de luxe way in Paris; and I along with all the literary set had discovered him, which was fun; and when he returned to New York we preached the new style and peculiar feeling of his fiction as if it were evangel. Still, that was too slow a start of a great career to suit Fitzgerald. Obviously Ernest was the one true genius of our decade, he said; and yet he was neglected and misunderstood and, above all, insufficiently remunerated. He thought I would agree that

The Apple of the Eye and *The Great Gatsby* were rather inflated market values just then. What could I do to help launch Hemingway? Why didn't I write a laudatory essay on him? With this questioning, Fitzgerald now and then impatiently grasped and shook my elbow.

There was something more than ordinary art-admiration about it, but on the other hand it was no mere matter of affection for Hemingway; it was so bold, unabashed, lacking in sense of humor. . . . I was touched and flattered by Fitzgerald's taking so much for granted. It simply had not occurred to him that unfriendliness or pettiness on my part might inhibit my enthusiasm about the art of a new colleague and rival.

In the spring of 1926 Fitzgerald, in accordance with his own advice to Wescott, wrote an article for *The Bookman* in which he conducted a rapid survey of World War I novels that had appeared since the beginning of the decade. E. E. Cummings' *The Enormous Room* would survive, thought Fitzgerald, "because those few who cause books to live have not been able to endure the thought of its mortality." Two other books—*Through the Wheat* and *Three Soldiers*—though imperfect in various ways, had permanent value. And that was all. However, Fitzgerald wrote, "as an augury that someone has profited by this dismal record of high hope and stale failure comes the first work of Ernest Hemingway." Fitzgerald followed this comment with a brief and highly favorable review of *In Our Time*. The review concludes: "It is sufficient that here is no raw food served up by the railroad restaurants of California and Wisconsin. In the best of these dishes there is not a bit to spare. And many of us who have grown weary of admonitions to 'watch this man or that' have felt a sort of renewal of excitement at these stories wherein Ernest Hemingway turns a corner into the street."

Hemingway had indeed entered the street, and it was to

lead him to destinations unsuspected even in Fitzgerald's imagination. His journey, like Fitzgerald's, had its beginning in the Middle Western United States. Born a few years apart near the close of the century, both authors had responded early to the impulse to leave the provincial world of their childhood.

Hemingway's college, as Carlos Baker has remarked, was the continent of Europe. His course of study included art and languages, people, politics, and war. Hemingway had been wounded in battle, had been decorated by the Italian Government, and had served an intensive apprenticeship as a foreign correspondent during the early years of the decade. In 1922, he had struck up a friendship with Gertrude Stein in Paris, where during the same period he also met James Joyce and Ezra Pound. Like Fitzgerald at Princeton, Hemingway was learning valuable lessons in the art of writing from his association with experienced practitioners of the craft.[1]

In the summer of 1923 Hemingway had collected some of his early work under the title *Three Stories and Ten Poems*, which was published by Robert McAlmon's Contact Publishing Company. The next year William Bird's Three Mountains Press brought out the young writer's *in our time*, which consisted of the vignettes or miniatures later incorporated into *In Our Time*. The critical reception of these two early works was meager; but Edmund Wilson published a favorable review in *The Dial* for October, 1924, which called attention to the influence of Gertrude Stein on the two volumes, but stressed as well the new writer's originality and importance. Wilson felt that *in our time* had more "artistic dignity" than anything written by an American

---

[1] For full biographical data see Charles A. Fenton, *The Apprenticeship of Ernest Hemingway* (New York, 1958) and Carlos Baker, *Hemingway* (Princeton, 1956).

about the period of the war. Earlier that year Wilson had shown *in our time* to Fitzgerald, had confided to him his enthusiasm for the new writer, and had urged Fitzgerald, who was planning a trip to Europe, to look up Hemingway on his arrival in Paris.

Hemingway, meanwhile, had returned to the United States with his family in the autumn of 1923, intending to establish himself, at least temporarily, as a member of the reporting staff on the *Toronto Star*. At this time he was undecided whether he should commit himself to the uncertain financial propects of a writing career. A number of unpleasant experiences at the *Star* during this period helped him make up his mind. After four months he left Toronto to return to Paris.

Hemingway devoted the year 1924 to hard work at his writing and to informal services as manuscript scout and part-time editor of Ford Madox Ford's *transatlantic review*. Several of Hemingway's short stories appeared in this magazine during 1924-1925 (they were later included in the collection *In Our Time*). Other expatriate journals had begun to accept the author's short fiction, and his reputation had begun to make itself felt among writers and editors in America. Edward O'Brien had selected one of his stories for inclusion in the anthology *The Best Short Stories of 1923*. Early in 1925, Boni and Liveright, acting on recommendations by O'Brien and Sherwood Anderson, offered Hemingway a contract for *In Our Time,* which was published late in the same year.

Hemingway thus made his initial appearance before American readers five years after Fitzgerald had attained high success with the publication of *This Side of Paradise*. When the two authors met in the autumn of 1924, Fitzgerald was an established author; his short stories commanded large sums from the slick American magazines; he had published two successful novels and had recently completed *The Great Gatsby,* which was scheduled to appear in the spring of 1925. Fitzgerald was, in fact, at the height of his fame and creative vigor. Hemingway had by that time acquired a limited reputation as an extremely promising author, and he was about to make his first appearance before an American audience. Fitzgerald had just turned twenty-eight. Hemingway was twenty-five.

In Paris, then as now, the place to meet people, to talk business, politics, and art is the café. In the summer of 1925, Fitzgerald and Hemingway enjoyed a good many such café discussions, with talk of art predominating. Christian Gauss, who was present on some of these occasions, remembered a conversation about Robert Louis Stevenson's advice to the young writer to "play the sedulous ape" to an experienced author until, in due time, the novice has developed a style of his own. Fitzgerald admitted that Compton Mackenzie had strongly influenced *This Side of Paradise,* and Hemingway said that *Winesburg, Ohio* had been his first model. "But both agreed," Gauss wrote later, "that you had to pay for whatever help this sort of imitation gave you in your apprenticeship. It was like consulting a psychiatrist. If you were to go on your own, you soon had to wean yourself of such outside direction."

At other meetings that summer Fitzgerald and Hemingway talked shop, argued aesthetics (as they were to do years later), and offered each other advice on work in progress. Gauss recalled a lively dispute in which he and Fitzgerald accused Hemingway of having written a story in which nothing happened. Hemingway replied that they had read the piece carelessly and had made no attempt to understand his intention. The story was "Big Two Hearted River," which had appeared a few months earlier in Ernest Walsh's *This Quarter*.

In "Ring," Fitzgerald wrote how a few years earlier he and Lardner had "tucked a lot under their belts in many weathers. . . ." No doubt the same pastime extended into the relationship with Hemingway, judging from the latter's portrait of his new friend in *The Torrents of Spring*: "It was at this point in the story, reader, that Mr. F. Scott Fitzgerald came to our home one afternoon, and after remaining for quite a while suddenly sat down in the fireplace and would not (or was it could not, reader?) get up and let the fire burn something else to keep the room warm." Sportive as this might sound, it is important to note that both Fitzgerald and Hemingway looked upon their friendship as more than casual; it was compounded in these early years not only of respect and affection, but of professional trust and affinity. A comment made years later by Christian Gauss supports this impression: "Though Hemingway was unknown in wider literary circles, he was closer to Scott at that time than any of the other young American writers in Paris."

During this summer of 1925, Fitzgerald was working on "The Rich Boy," one of his most perfectly realized short stories on the subject of the wealthy class in America. Fitzgerald showed this story to Hemingway while it was still in manuscript, and Hemingway gave it high praise. But more significant than this personal exchange is the very strong possibility that "The Rich Boy" was written, in part, under the influence of Hemingway's prose style. Years later —in 1936—Fitzgerald claimed that he had not imitated Hemingway's "infectious style." "My own style," he said "such as it is, was formed before he published anything." But in 1934, Fitzgerald admitted in a letter to Hemingway: "There are pieces and paragraphs of your work that I read

over and over—in fact, I stopped myself doing it for a year
and a half because I was afraid that your particular rhythms
were going to creep in on mine by a process of infiltration."
Passages in "The Rich Boy" suggest that this process was
already in operation in 1925. The influence of the famous
Hemingway manner is all the more conspicuous, in fact,
for its being so completely uncharacteristic of Fitzgerald's
work up to that time.

Near the end of "The Rich Boy" Anson Hunter, Fitzgerald's hero, visits Paula Legendre, a former sweetheart
whom he has not seen in seven years. Paula is now married,
and Fitzgerald has Anson witness a playful scene between
Paula and her husband which reveals the security and affection that fill her life. At the same time the scene strikes
home to Anson Hunter the realization of what he has
missed by his casual and egocentric attitude toward Paula
several years earlier:

> Hagerty [Paula's husband] came in a little before eleven;
> after a whiskey Paula stood up and announced that she was
> going to bed. She went over and stood by her husband.
> "Where did you go, dearest?" she demanded.
> "I had a drink with Ed Saunders."
> "I was worried. I thought maybe you'd run away."
> She rested her head against his coat.
> "He's sweet, isn't he, Anson?" she demanded.
> "Absolutely," said Anson, laughing.
> She raised her face to her husband.
> "Well, I'm ready," she said. She turned to Anson: "Do
> you want to see our family gymnastic stunt?"
> "Yes," he said in an interested voice.
> "All right. Here we go!"
> Hagerty picked her up easily in his arms.
> "This is called the family acrobatic stunt," said Paula.
> "He carries me up-stairs. Isn't it sweet of him?"

"Yes," said Anson.

Hagerty bent his head slightly until his face touched Paula's.

"And I love him," she said. "I've just been telling you, haven't I, Anson?"

"Yes," he said.

"He's the dearest thing that ever lived in this world; aren't you, darling? . . . Well, good night. Here we go. Isn't he strong?"

"Yes," Anson said.

"You'll find a pair of Pete's pajamas laid out for you. Sweet dreams—see you at breakfast."

"Yes," Anson said.

The formula should be familiar to readers of Ernest Hemingway. Anson Hunter's monosyllabic replies suggest by a virtually absolute simplicity the depth of his emotion. But if the passage does reflect Hemingway's influence, it is of minor significance; a later section of this chapter will consider more important aspects of the subject. I call attention here to the episode in "The Rich Boy" only to indicate the way in which Fitzgerald's friendship with Hemingway was already, in 1925, leaving its mark on his work.

While Fitzgerald was finishing "The Rich Boy," Hemingway had begun work on *The Sun Also Rises*, which was to occupy him during the summer and autumn of 1925. According to Arthur Mizener, Hemingway showed Fitzgerald an early draft of this novel, and they "discussed it at great length." Later, Hemingway reported further progress in a letter to Fitzgerald: "I cut The Sun to start with Cohn—cut all that first part. made a number of minor cuts and did quite a lot of re-writing and tightening up. . . . in proof it read[s] like a good book. . . . I hope to hell you'll like it and I think maybe you will."

Just before *The Sun Also Rises* was published, Fitzgerald

sent Maxwell Perkins a careful estimate of Hemingway's novel and a plea for special consideration: "I liked it but with certain qualifications. The fiesta, the fishing trip, the minor characters were fine. The lady [Brett] I didn't like, perhaps because I don't like the original. . . . Do ask him for the absolute minimum of necessary changes, Max—he's so discouraged about the previous reception of his work by publishers and magazine editors."

Both Fitzgerald and Hemingway kept continually on the move during the years 1926-1930; rarely did either one settle in one place for more than a few months. Yet they continued to correspond, and they always managed to see each other when their paths crossed. In 1927, Hemingway showed Fitzgerald the manuscript of a story he was writing entitled "Fifty Grand"; Fitzgerald recommended cutting some early parts of the story, to which advice Hemingway, apparently, agreed. And late in 1928 or early in 1929, Hemingway sent Fitzgerald a draft of *A Farewell to Arms,* asking for an opinion on the ending, about which Hemingway was still in doubt. Fitzgerald claimed later that he "worked like hell on the idea" (that is, on a possible conclusion for *A Farewell to Arms*), but could not satisfy Hemingway's notion of "what an ending should be." Some time later, in fact, Hemingway argued so persuasively his own ideas on the subject that Fitzgerald let himself be guided by his friend's judgment when he came to write the ending of *Tender Is the Night.* "You felt that the true line of a work of fiction," Fitzgerald wrote Hemingway soon after he had finished the novel, "was to take a reader up to a high emotional pitch but then let him down or ease him off. You gave no aesthetic reason for this—nevertheless, you convinced me." In such ways did these two authors effect minor but indelible impressions on each other's works.

The late nineteen-twenties and early thirties was a time,

as we have seen in earlier chapters, when Fitzgerald's confidence was badly undermined by a number of personal crises and a seemingly unshakable artistic inertia. His relations with his friends suffered too, from attrition and a tendency on Fitzgerald's part to pick quarrels over imagined insults. In 1929, Fitzgerald wrote in his Notebooks that Hemingway had begun to be "cold" toward him. He also wrote a letter to Hemingway criticizing what he called the latter's "superior attitude." And there was an episode involving a boxing match between Hemingway and Morley Callaghan, with Fitzgerald presiding as referee, which ended in misunderstanding and general unpleasantness. Throughout these uneasy misadventures Hemingway played the part of peacemaker; yet Fitzgerald had been gradually developing the idea, which was to grow worse before it grew better, that he was a failure and that Ernest Hemingway was a success—that his own career was in decline while Hemingway's was in the ascendant. "I talk with the authority of failure—" Fitzgerald commented sometime during this period, "Ernest with the authority of success. We could never sit across the same table again." This was no mere petulance on Fitzgerald's part: he had failed to produce a novel for a number of years, and he must have been aware of the critical and popular success of A *Farewell to Arms*.

In addition, Hemingway had begun to be severely critical of Fitzgerald's drinking. Hemingway was also convinced, as H. L. Mencken had been some years earlier, that Fitzgerald's life with Zelda was destructive to his artistic development: "Of all people on earth," he wrote Fitzgerald in 1934, "you need discipline in your work and instead you marry someone who is jealous of your work, wants to compete with you and ruins you. It's not as simple as that and I thought Zelda was crazy the first time I met her and you complicated it even more by being in love with her and, of course you're a rummy." Such were the complications that had entered into the relationship between the two writers. They help to explain Fitzgerald's uneasiness in Hemingway's company: "With Ernest I seem to have reached a state where when we drink together I half bait, half truckle to him," Fitzgerald wrote to his friend Edmund Wilson.

During these years, too, Fitzgerald seems to have suffered some guilt over his failure to live up to what Hemingway called "artistic conscience." Hemingway had expressed his views on this subject repeatedly: he felt that the writer of fiction must be dedicated to an ideal of excellence that can survive all temptations to compromise his artistic standards. Hemingway's thumbnail portrait of a hypothetical writer of great prose in *Green Hills of Africa* includes this kind of integrity as a requisite: "First, there must be talent. Talent such as Kipling had. Then there must be discipline. The discipline of Flaubert. Then there must be the conception of what it can be and an absolute conscience as unchanging as the standard meter in Paris, to prevent faking." The forces that militate against the writer's artistic conscience, Hemingway believed, are the debilitating self-indulgences such as excessive drinking and the desire for comfort and luxury.

"You see we make our writers into something very strange" [says the narrator of *Green Hills of Africa*].
"We destroy them in many ways. First, economically. They make money. It is only by hazard that a writer makes money although good books always make money eventually. Then our writers when they have made some money increase their standard of living and they are caught. They have to write to keep up their establishments, their wives, and so on, and they write slop. It is slop not on purpose but because it is hurried. Because they write when there is nothing to say or no water in the well. Because they are

ambitious. Then, once they have betrayed themselves, they
justify it and you get more slop."

In the back of his mind, perhaps, Hemingway was
directing these remarks obliquely at Fitzgerald. Later,
in "The Snows of Kilimanjaro," he was to expand the theme
into a memorable work of fiction, at the same time that he
made the reference to Fitzgerald more explicit. But there
is no doubt that Hemingway's comments on the corrupting
forces that ruin the artist impressed themselves on Fitzgerald's imagination. In his Notebooks, the latter wrote:
"Nevertheless, value of Ernest's feeling about the pure
heart when writing—in other words, the comparatively pure
heart, the 'house in order.'" A few years later in his introduction for the Modern Library edition of *The Great
Gatsby* Fitzgerald revealed that he had seriously considered
the concept of "artistic conscience" as it applied to his own
work. Never, Fitzgerald remarked, had he tried so hard
to preserve his artistic conscience as during the ten months
when he was writing *Gatsby*. "If there is a clear conscience,"
he said, "a book can survive. . . ." But even more to the
point is Fitzgerald's comment in "The Crack-Up," when he is
making a list of the men who influenced him most
strongly: "A third contemporary had been an artistic conscience to me," Fitzgerald wrote; and there can be no doubt
that he meant Ernest Hemingway, and that Hemingway had
become to him in his moments of doubt and weakness a
symbol of artistic integrity.

He had also become the ultimate judge and arbiter of
Fitzgerald's ability. To Maxwell Perkins, Fitzgerald wrote
in 1934 that Hemingway had pointed out some superfluous
sections of *Tender Is the Night* and that as an artist
Hemingway was as close to being a final reference as anyone Fitzgerald knew. Around the same time Fitzgerald

wrote to Hemingway: "I think it is obvious that my respect for your artistic life is absolutely unqualified, that save for a few of the dead or dying old men you are the only man writing fiction in America that I look up to very much."

Still, it would be a mistake to overemphasize Fitzgerald's dependence on Hemingway's judgments, aesthetic or otherwise. An exchange of letters shortly after the release of *Tender Is the Night* demonstrates Fitzgerald's faith, for example, in his own ideas concerning the dynamics of character-making in fiction. Hemingway wrote a long, serious letter criticizing his friend's treatment of the major characters in the novel, claiming in particular that Fitzgerald had created inconsistent impressions by fusing several characters from real life. Fitzgerald replied by citing Shakespeare's habit of combining contemporary themes with information from Plutarch and Holinshed. Thus, to Fitzgerald, composite characterization was perfectly possible to execute successfully, though he did admit that perhaps he had not brought it off so well in *Tender Is the Night*. Fitzgerald's reply seems not to answer Hemingway's objections exactly; but the exchange at the very least shows that Fitzgerald stood by his own ideas and was not invariably swayed by Hemingway's opinions.

The mood of depression, however, deepened during the years following the publication of *Tender Is the Night*. Fitzgerald's financial problems, his wife's hopeless mental collapse, and his dwindling popularity all contributed to the condition of spirit which he delineated with such merciless candor in "The Crack-Up," a series of three articles written for *Esquire* in 1935. "The conjurer's hat was empty," said Fitzgerald in one of these articles. "To draw things out of it had long been a sort of sleight of hand, and now, to change the metaphor, I was off the dispensing end of the relief roll forever." The series concludes: "the sign *Cave*

Canem is hung permanently just above my door. I will try to be a correct animal though, and if you throw me a bone with enough meat on it I may even lick your hand."

The response of Fitzgerald's close friends to this public confession only added to his troubles. Edmund Wilson objected to Fitzgerald that he had revealed too much of himself in the series. John Dos Passos wrote a letter in which he tried to encourage Fitzgerald to apply himself to a long work of fiction; but he could not resist adding: "Christ, man, how do you find time in the middle of the general conflagration to worry about all that stuff? . . . . We're living in one of the damnedest tragic moments in history—if you want to go to pieces I think it's absolutely O. K. but I think you ought to write a first rate novel about it (and you probably will) instead of spilling it in little pieces for Arnold Gingrich. . . ."

But the greatest disparagement came from Ernest Hemingway, who in a letter to Maxwell Perkins expressed his disgust at Fitzgerald's self-revelation: it was really miserable, said Hemingway, for Fitzgerald to whine in public; Fitzgerald was in senility, had by-passed his manhood completely; a writer ought to quell his cowardice and write. But what hurt Fitzgerald most was the by now famous reference in "The Snows of Kilimanjaro," which appeared in *Esquire* only a few months after "The Crack-Up":

> He remembered poor Scott Fitzgerald and his romantic awe of [the rich] and how he had started a story once that began "The very rich are different from you and me." And how some one said to Scott, Yes, they have more money. But that was not humorous to Scott. He thought they were a special glamorous race and when he found out they weren't it wrecked him just as much as any other thing that wrecked him.

The reference is even more pointed in the context of the

story, which concerns a would-be writer who has destroyed his talent by surrendering to dissipation and the love of luxury. Later, when Hemingway heard about Fitzgerald's injured reaction, he changed the name from "poor Scott Fitzgerald" to "poor Julian," and that is the way it now appears when the story is anthologized. But at the time, "The Snows of Kilimanjaro" must have seemed to Fitzgerald a completely gratuitous but unmistakable assault on his way of life. "Ernest claimed he was free to write that way about me because of what I'd written about myself," Fitzgerald told Sheilah Graham a few years later. "I don't think I can ever forgive him. That was hitting me when I was down." And in a mood of unhappy reminiscence he entered in his Notebooks: "Ernest—until we began trying to walk over each other with cleats."

The middle and late thirties—which for Fitzgerald were artistically unproductive years—he spent in Hollywood drawing large salaries but otherwise pursued by frustration and bad luck. The good work he did for the Hollywood studios was either revised and cheapened by his producer, or permanently shelved. Aside from the brilliant writing of "The Crack-Up," Fitzgerald published only a few short stories that possessed the old distinction ("Design in Plaster" and "The Lost Decade") and one or two essays of more than passing interest ("Afternoon of an Author" and "Early Success"); in addition, the royalties from his books still in print had sunk to virtually nothing. These circumstances must have intensified his growing feeling that he was engaged in a kind of private competition with Ernest Hemingway, with the latter winning all the honors.

A number of incidents seemed to encourage this impression. T. S. Eliot, for example, had sent Scribner's a statement to be used on the dust jacket of *Tender Is the Night:* "I have been waiting impatiently for another book by Mr.

Scott Fitzgerald," Eliot wrote, "with more eagerness and curiosity than I should feel towards the work of any of his contemporaries except that of Mr. Ernest Hemingway." Fitzgerald's story price, too, had sunk to two hundred and fifty dollars (Hemingway's sports sketches for the same magazine brought twice that amount). With some bitterness, Fitzgerald wrote Arnold Gingrich, asking him to publish his most recent story under a pseudonym: he was tired of being Scott Fitzgerald, the novelist said; there was no money in it these days. This from the writer whose stories in the good years had sold for four thousand dollars each.

During this period Fitzgerald was also trying to persuade Maxwell Perkins to reissue *This Side of Paradise*. Soon after Scribner's published Hemingway's *The Fifth Column and the First Forty-Nine Stories*, Fitzgerald wrote Perkins inquiring casually whether Hemingway's sales were good or bad and adding that he himself was beginning to feel badly neglected. He was afraid, he confided to Perkins, that his reputation was "slipping away." Edmund Wilson, sensing Fitzgerald's hopelessness, sent repeated messages of encouragement assuring him that he could still catch up with Hemingway. Though Hemingway's stories were excellent, said Wilson, "now is your time to creep up on him." But in a despairing mood in the late thirties Fitzgerald confessed to a friend "I don't write any more. Ernest has made all my writing unnecessary."

But the old admiration for what Fitzgerald called Hemingway's "Byronic intensity" continued undiminished. Fitzgerald wrote in his Notebooks: "As to Ernest as a boy: reckless, adventurous, etc. Yet it is undeniable that the dark was peopled for him. His bravery and acquired characteristics." And from 1934 until the end of his life Fitzgerald was engaged in writing installments of "The Count of Darkness," a melodrama set in the middle ages, which he referred to in his Notebooks as "the story of Ernest." Its hero, Phillipe, is based on Hemingway's character—or at least on Hemingway's nobility and heroism, as conceived by Fitzgerald. "The Count of Darkness" was never completed, which is probably just as well: it is poor stuff compared to the best of Fitzgerald's work. But its concentration on Phillipe—"a leader of men" who is "possessed by a psychology that delighted in toughness for its own sake" —shows us how much Hemingway must have filled Fitzgerald's thoughts during these years. "The Count of Darkness" also provides evidence that despite his strained relations with Hemingway, Fitzgerald never lost his fascination with his friend's dramatic personality.

Fitzgerald's admiration for Hemingway, in fact, prevailed over his injured pride, his sense of defeat and betrayal, and the damage his ego had suffered at Hemingway's hands. One of the last letters Fitzgerald wrote—just a little over a month before his death—was to Hemingway, thanking him for sending on an inscribed copy of *For Whom the Bell Tolls*. Fitzgerald said he read the novel with intense interest, participating in some of the writing problems and fully appreciating Hemingway's skill in solving them. "It's a fine novel," Fitzgerald commented, "better than anybody else writing could do." And: "Congratulations too on your new book's great success. I envy you like hell and there is no irony in this." Fitzgerald closed the letter "With old affection. . . ."

Perhaps the best way to summarize this brief history of the Fitzgerald-Hemingway companionship is to return to Glenway Wescott's essay "The Moral of Scott Fitzgerald." Wescott, it will be remembered, stressed Fitzgerald's excitement over the promising talent of the young Ernest

Hemingway who was just then emerging from obscurity. But "The Moral of Scott Fitzgerald" contains another impression—perhaps a crucial one—of Fitzgerald's attitude:

> He not only said, but, I believe, honestly felt that Hemingway was inimitably, essentially superior. From the moment Hemingway began to appear in print, perhaps it did not matter what he himself produced or failed to produce. He felt free to write just for profit, and to live for fun, if possible. Hemingway could be entrusted with the graver responsibilities and higher rewards such as glory, immortality. This extreme of admiration—this excuse for a morbid belittlement and abandonment of himself—was bad for Fitzgerald, I imagine. At all events he soon began to waste his energy in various hack-writing.

Was Fitzgerald's attachment to Hemingway, then, an unfortunate factor in his personal and professional decline? Perhaps so, though it is unlikely that Hemingway was a willing agent in the gradual disaster. Hemingway's attitude throughout the relationship was no doubt too complicated to understand fully—at least on the basis of the evidence now available. He certainly felt the strong appeal of Fitzgerald's talent, sincerity, and personal attractiveness. Yet the spirit of disregard which prompted his public expression of scorn for his bedeviled colleague was strong, too—strong enough, perhaps, to have been dominant. Hemingway's last remarks on Fitzgerald, published twenty years after the latter's death, sound the old note of bullying contempt: "Fitzgerald was soft," Hemingway told a feature writer for *Holiday* magazine in 1960. "He dissolved at the least touch of alcohol." Hemingway added that he had no patience with writers who operated in "saucedom."

This is an odd, though perhaps not altogether surprising, tribute to pay fifteen years of friendship. But whatever other memories Hemingway could have evoked remained unspoken.

II

As with the personal relations between Fitzgerald and Hemingway, so with the relationship between the works they produced: they seem close and yet distant, at times full of affinities and correspondences, at other times dissimilar, virtually irreconcilable. For years critics and literary historians have linked the names of these two writers, frequently associating them as members of the same movement, as spokesmen for the values of a "lost generation," and as practitioners of similar novelistic techniques, moods, and themes. Yet a statement made by Christian Gauss, quoted by Carlos Baker in his study of Hemingway, suggests a fundamental disparity that must be reckoned with: "Fitzgerald was, and remained, an earnest and competent student of the art of writing, and this was one of the bonds between Scott and Hemingway," said Gauss, speaking of Fitzgerald and Hemingway in the mid-twenties. "In other respects," he added, "they were worlds apart. Hemingway was not interested in the Ritz or playboys. His special interest lay in the more exacting forms of physical proficiency and courage." Professor Baker, too, implies that these two authors differ essentially, at least in their treatments of one major theme. "It is almost as if, throughout the depression," says Baker, "Hemingway had resolutely set himself to oppose F. Scott Fitzgerald's temperamental conviction that the rich are glamorous." And Alfred Kazin, in a discussion of Hemingway, Dos Passos, and Fitzgerald, claims that "Fitzgerald, who never underwent the European apprenticeship the others did, always stood rather apart from them, though he was the historian of his generation and for a long time its most famous symbol." These few comments hardly represent a unified body of critical opinion; yet they suggest the unlikely prospect of discovering any clear-cut parallels in the novels and stories of these two writers.

It is extremely difficult, for example, to make any conclusive comments on the matter of influences operating between Fitzgerald and Hemingway, though influences there surely are, as we shall see presently. For the moment, however, a comparison of certain passages from these two writers will bring to light the themes they had in common and the basic similarities and differences in their perspectives. The comparative readings that follow should also indicate that the remarks made by Gauss, Baker, and Kazin overemphasize the differences between Fitzgerald and Hemingway and need modification.

Fitzgerald and Hemingway have their closest points of affinity in three themes which figure prominently in their works during the nineteen-twenties and early thirties. These themes I shall designate the alien outsider, the modern woman, and the ruined writer. All three reflect actual events and attitudes in modern American experience; and all three were treated by other contemporary writers. The first of these motifs, the alien outsider, underlies Fitzgerald's treatment of Meyer Wolfsheim in *The Great Gatsby* and Hemingway's portrayal of Robert Cohn in *The Sun Also Rises*. Our understanding of these two fictional characters will be enriched by a brief consideration of the social fabric out of which they emerged.

The vein of anti-Semitism that runs through the literature of the nineteen-twenties is symptomatic of the national attitude, and symbolic in its function. It is perhaps related to the strong antipathy toward aliens that gathered force during the period and that found expression in such incidents as the Palmer raids, the rise of the Ku Klux Klan, and the execution of Sacco and Vanzetti. Liberals and intellectuals of the time agreed in their interpretation of these events, at least in certain important particulars. The general feeling against foreigners and minority groups was economic in origin, they claimed, and prejudice in America was based on a fear that the minority might injure the majority's material interests. So speak two of the essayists who appear in the omnibus *Civilization in the United States*.

But the anti-Semitism in the fiction and poetry of the period was based on a threat not to the pocketbook, but to the social structure. Here was another aspect of the breakdown in class distinctions, another indication of the rise of the *nouveau riche*; but in this case the enterprising social aspirer was disqualified not only by a deficiency in manners or background, but by virtue also of his alleged "racial" characteristics. T. S. Eliot's well-known poem "Burbank with a Baedeker: Bleistein with a Cigar" will serve as an illustration:

> But this or such was Bleistein's way:
>   A saggy bending of the knees
> And elbows, with the palms turned out,
>   Chicago Semite Viennese.
>
> A lustreless protrusive eye
>   Stares from the protozoic slime
> At a perspective of Canaletto.
>   The smoky candle end of time
>
> Declines. On the Rialto once.
>   The rats are underneath the piles.
> The jew is underneath the lot.
>   Money in furs. The boatman smiles. . . .

What disturbs Eliot is not the fact that Bleistein is a Jew, but that now, in a world of social disorder and instability, Bleistein has pretensions to culture: the "Chicago Semite" has invaded the museums to gape at a perspective of Canaletto. An episode in Sinclair Lewis's *Dodsworth* brings into even sharper focus the social pattern Eliot deplores in "Burbank with a Baedeker." During her travels in Europe, Fran Dodsworth engages in a flirtation with the penniless Count von Obersdorf, who tells her at one point of the peculiar situation of one of his friends, the Archduke Michael. The Archduke, it seems, has taken employment as a chauffeur to a Hungarian Jew. The Jew in the fiction of the twenties is not only, in Eliot's phrase, "underneath the lot." He is also, what is more distressing, at the top of the ladder! The Jew in a prominent position was to the writers of the postwar decade a symbol of the world turned upside down.

These considerations help to elucidate Hemingway's treatment of Robert Cohn in *The Sun Also Rises*. Cohn's schooling and his relation with his classmates, for example, parallel the actual assault on hitherto "sacrosanct" institutions:

> Robert Cohn was a member, through his father, of one of the richest Jewish families in New York, and through his mother of one of the oldest. At the military school where he prepped for Princeton, and played a very good end on the football team, no one had made him race-conscious. No one had ever made him feel he was a Jew, and hence any different from anybody else, until he went to Princeton.

In the figure of Robert Cohn, however, Hemingway has not attempted to create a stereotype of the totally unattractive intruder represented by Eliot's Bleistein. Cohn is, in Jake's words, "a nice boy, a friendly boy, and very shy. . . . I rather liked him. . . ." He is also quite individual—a human, rather than an abstract portrait—with his peculiar mixture of naïveté and devotion to Jake and Brett, his ability to withstand insults and humiliation, his prize-fighter physical strength and his, at times, unmanly weakness of character. It is quite reasonable, in fact, to think of Cohn as a combination of extreme qualities—both unattractive and attractive—someone who is easy to hate and easy to be fond of, by turns likable aind contemptible. The poker-dice image near the end of the novel seems to suggest this ambivalence in Jake's attitude toward Robert Cohn: "So we rolled poker dice out of a deep leather dice-cup. . . . On the final roll Mike had three kings, an ace, and a queen." The queen here might represent Brett Ashley, the three kings Jake Barnes, Bill Gorton, and Mike Campbell (three of a kind—members of the exclusive café-table fellowship). And the ace, which may stand in poker as either the highest or the lowest quantity, is Robert Cohn.

But if Hemingway has made Cohn a convincingly human rather than a stereotyped character, he has also suggested in Cohn's behavior the pattern of the unwanted outsider trying to identify himself with a class to which he does not belong. Even in the early sections of the novel, when Jake's feelings toward Cohn are friendly and sympathetic, there are indications that Jake does not consider him, in Brett's significant phrase, "one of us." Cohn is romantic rather than cynical; he accepts insults passively; and he has a "hard, Jewish, stubborn streak."

But Jake Barnes and his circle of ultrasophisticated friends resent most of all Cohn's calfish devotion to the titled beauty Brett Ashley; and Brett's alcoholic fiancé expresses this resentment in an ugly emotional scene just before the start of the Pamplona festival:

"What if Brett did sleep with you?" [Mike asks Robert Cohn.] "She's slept with lots of better people than you."
"Shut up," Cohn said. He stood up. "Shut up, Mike."

"Oh, don't stand up and act as though you were going to hit me. That won't make any difference to me. Tell me, Robert. Why do you follow Brett around like a poor bloody steer? Don't you know you're not wanted? I know when I'm not wanted. Why don't you know when you're not wanted? You came down to San Sebastian where you weren't wanted, and followed Brett around like a bloody steer. Do you think that's right?"

"Shut up. You're drunk."

"Perhaps I am drunk. Why aren't you drunk? Why don't you ever get drunk, Robert? You know you didn't have a good time at San Sebastian because none of our friends would invite you on any of the parties. You can't blame them hardly. Can you? I asked them to. They wouldn't do it. You can't blame them, now. Can you? Now, answer me. Can you blame them?"

The impression we receive of Cohn at this point is complicated by the fact that it is Mike Campbell—presented throughout as a tactless man of weak character—who makes these abusive statements I have quoted. Yet in the passage immediately following, after Cohn has been led off by Bill Gorton, Hemingway implies that Mike speaks for the fellowship of "insiders" represented by Brett, Jake Barnes, and Mike Campbell:

"I say, Michael, you might not be such a bloody ass," Brett interrupted. "I'm not saying he's not right, you know." She turned to me.

The emotion left Mike's voice. We were all friends together.

"I'm not so damn drunk as I sounded," he said.

"I know you're not," Brett said.

"We're none of us sober," I said.

"I didn't say anything I didn't mean."

"But you put it so badly," Brett laughed.

"He was an ass, though. He came down to San Sebastian

where he damn well wasn't wanted. He hung around Brett and just *looked* at her. It made me damned well sick."

"He did behave very badly," Brett said.

"Mark you. Brett's had affairs with men before. She tells me everything. She gave me this chap Cohn's letters to read. I wouldn't read them."

"Damned noble of you."

"No, listen, Jake. Brett's gone off with men. But they weren't ever Jews, and they didn't come and hang about afterward."

Milton Hindus, in an essay published in *Commentary* in 1947, has remarked that the anti-Semitism of such writers of the nineteen-twenties as Eliot, Hemingway, and Fitzgerald is "literary anti-Semitism"—it reflects a feeling of social distaste, rather than a personal hatred of the Jew. Hemingway's portrait of Robert Cohn conforms to this definition in a curious way. The resentment Hemingway's characters display toward Cohn may be taken symbolically, as the resentment of an established class against an upstart alien; but their antipathy is also more concrete, the result of a clash of personalities and emotional conflicts that arise irrespective of Cohn's status as a Jew. Hemingway's purpose in making Cohn a Jew is to add a dimension of social comment to his novel; but that purpose, it would seem, is secondary to his interest in human character. Cohn is a three-dimensional figure, and a memorable one, a skillfully delineated dramatis persona. This is perhaps a significant clue to the difference between Robert Cohn and Wolfsheim in Fitzgerald's *The Great Gatsby*.

It would be difficult, for example, to imagine anyone paying Hemingway a compliment such as Fitzgerald received from Edith Wharton. "It's enough to make this reader happy," wrote Mrs. Wharton soon after she had read *The Great Gatsby*, "to have met your perfect Jew, &

the limp Wilson, & assisted at that seedy orgy in the Buchanan flat, with the dazed puppy looking on. Every bit of that is masterly—but the lunch with Hildeshiem [Wolfsheim] and his every appearance afterward, make me augur still greater things!"

Mrs. Wharton's comment is best understood as a reflection of that attitude, shared by other writers of the period, which conceived of the Jew as a symbol of social disruption. Wolfsheim is a "perfect" Jew in the sense that he fulfills the symbolic and stereotyped image of the upstart alien without the complication of redeeming or human qualities, such as we have seen in Hemingway's portrait of Robert Cohn. A brief look at Wolfsheim will clearly illustrate this difference.

Nick Carraway's initial impression of Meyer Wolfsheim suggests Fitzgerald's intention to caricature rather than to characterize: "A small, flat-nosed Jew raised his large head and regarded me with two fine growths of hair which luxuriated in either nostril. After a moment I discovered his tiny eyes in the half-darkness." At this first meeting, Wolfsheim indulges in a reminiscence concerning a friend whose evening meal was abruptly terminated:

"The old Metropole," brooded Mr. Wolfsheim gloomily. "Filled with faces dead and gone. Filled with friends gone now forever. I can't forget so long as I live the night they shot Rosy Rosenthal there. It was six of us at the table, and Rosy had eat and drunk a lot all evening. When it was almost morning the waiter came up to him with a funny look and says somebody wants to speak to him outside. 'All right,' says Rosy, and begins to get up, and I pulled him down in his chair.

" 'Let the bastards come in here if they want you, Rosy, but don't you, so help me, move outside this room.'

". . . He turned around in the door and says: 'Don't let

that waiter take away my coffee!' Then he went out on the sidewalk, and they shot him three times in his full belly and drove away."

These ruminations have a curious relationship to Jay Gatsby. Wolfsheim's vulgar sentiment is a grotesque parallel to the hero's romantic nostalgia. Gatsby's mind, too, is filled "with faces dead and gone. Filled with friends gone now forever."

A little later in Fitzgerald's novel we learn that Wolfsheim is a gambler (his character, in fact, was based on the famous gambler of the twenties, Arnold Rothstein); he was responsible for "fixing" the World Series of 1919; and he is involved in a number of mysterious, but probably equally illegal, enterprises. "Why isn't he in jail?" asks Nick Carraway. "They can't get him, old sport," answers Jay Gatsby, crystallizing one of the basic attitudes of the prosperity decade. "He's a smart man."

Having invested Wolfsheim with the morals of a crook and the character and appearance of the typical alien outsider of the period, Fitzgerald adds to the over-all impression of distaste by having Wolfsheim speak in the idiom of the social climber: he is always telling Nick Carraway that Gatsby is a man of "fine breeding"—a "perfect gentleman"—"a college man." Fitzgerald also plays upon Wolfsheim's physiognomy by repeated reference to his "tragic nose," his "expressive nose"—"his nose flashed at me indignantly" and "his nostrils turned to me in an interested way." To round out the portrait there is Wolfsheim's accent: "I understand you're looking for a business gonnegtion"—"He went to Oggsford College in England. You know Oggsford College?" As the center of corruption in Fitzgerald's novel, as a vulgarly sentimental, prominent-nosed, ironical respecter of "breeding" and gentlemanliness, as an English-garbling immigrant Jew, Wolfsheim is indeed a "perfect" specimen. He is one with Eliot's Bleistein and the appalling flood of "fantastic neanderthals" Fitzgerald writes about in his essay "Echoes of the Jazz Age," in which he describes the American tourists in Europe who were "spewed up by the boom":

> . . . Toward the end there was something sinister about the boatloads. They were no longer the simple ma and pa and son and daughter, infinitely superior in their qualities of kindness and curiosity to the corresponding class in Europe, but fantastic neanderthals who believed something, something vague, that you remembered from a very cheap novel. I remember an Italian on a steamer who promenaded the deck in an American Reserve Officer's uniform picking quarrels in broken English with Americans who criticised their own institutions in the bar. I remember a fat Jewess, inlaid with diamonds, who sat behind us at the Russian ballet and said as the curtain rose, "Thad's luffly, dey ought to baint a bicture of it." This was low comedy, but it was evident that money and power were falling into the hands of people in comparison with whom the leader of a village Soviet would be a gold-mine of judgment and culture. There were citizens travelling in luxury in 1928 and 1929 who, in the distortion of their new condition, had the human value of Pekinese, bivalves, cretins, goats.

This is dehumanization with a vengeance!

But Fitzgerald's portrayal of Wolfsheim in *The Great Gatsby* and his remarks in "Echoes of the Jazz Age" constitute only one phase of the novelist's developing attitude toward the alien. In an earlier chapter I have called attention to Joseph Bloeckman of *The Beautiful and Damned,* who is represented as a type of the socially ambitious Jewish "outsider." Fitzgerald records Bloeckman's gradual ascent, it will be remembered, in a detached spirit of social observation. Bloeckman, like Wolfsheim in *The Great Gatsby,* serves a symbolic function; but unlike Wolfsheim he is in no sense a gross and unattractive caricature. It should be added, however, that Anthony Patch's attitude toward Bloeckman is full of resentment and distaste. Toward the end of the novel Anthony, who by this time has lost his income, his youth, and his conviction of superiority, pays Bloeckman a visit with the intention of borrowing money. On this occasion Bloeckman presents an emphatic contrast to the hero; he is prosperous and confident, calm and assured in his manner. In the scene that follows this confrontation of the dynamic *nouveau riche* and the disgruntled bankrupt, Anthony loses sight of his original purpose in seeking out Bloeckman, and accuses him (altogether unjustly) of an interest in Gloria, Anthony's wife:

> "Look here, Mr. Patch," said Bloeckman, evenly and without changing his expression, "you're drunk. You're disgustingly and insultingly drunk."
>
> "Not too drunk talk to you," insisted Anthony with a leer. "Firs' place, my wife wants nothin' whatever do with you. Never did. Un'erstand me?"
>
> "Be quiet!" said the older man angrily. "I should think you'd respect your wife enough not to bring her into the conversation under these circumstances."
>
> "Never you min' how I expect my wife. One thing—you leave her alone. You go to hell!"
>
> "See here—I think you're a little crazy!" exclaimed Bloeckman. He took two paces forward as though to pass by, but Anthony stepped in his way.
>
> "Not so fas', you Goddam Jew."

Just where Fitzgerald's sympathies lie in this encounter is difficult to say. He acknowledged to a friend that he was painting a self-portrait in the character of Anthony Patch; yet it is unlikely that he had any admiration for the Anthony Patch of the foregoing scene. It is more probable that Fitzgerald meant to portray Patch's anti-Semitism as a symptom of his deterioration. Years later, in *Tender Is the Night*, Fitzgerald has Dick Diver express similar racial or nationalistic intolerance to the same effect: Diver's use of the word "spic" and his open expressions of antipathy toward the English are calculated to suggest the disintegration of his character. Fitzgerald recognized in himself similar tendencies toward prejudice and identified them in 1936 as "inhuman and undernourished . . . the true sign of cracking up." In his worst hours, Fitzgerald wrote in "The Crack-Up," he couldn't stand the sight of Celts, English, Politicians, Strangers, Virginians, and Negroes (light or dark). It is probable, then, and worth emphasizing, that the antialien sentiment in *The Beautiful and Damned* and *Tender Is the Night* reflects the emotional condition of Fitzgerald's fictional heroes in their decline. In these two novels, at least, if not in *The Great Gatsby*, Fitzgerald is implying that such prejudice is contemptible and unhealthy.

But the final stage in the development of Fitzgerald's attitude toward this subject is seen in his presentation of Monroe Stahr, the man of dynamic personality and intellect who is the hero of *The Last Tycoon*. The fact that Stahr is a Jew, with the qualities of imagination and emotion Fitzgerald always admired, is an obvious instance of the author's having revised his stereotyped and unsympathetic conception of the Jew as expressed in the figure of Wolfsheim, and of his having achieved a more positive, less neutral attitude than that implied in the presentation of Bloeckman.

A number of factors might be mentioned to explain Fitzgerald's decision to make the hero of his last novel a Jew. For one thing, the novelist was deeply impressed by the highly respected young motion-picture producer Irving Thalberg, whom he met in Hollywood and upon whom he drew for his characterization of Monroe Stahr. Then, too, the atmosphere of anti-Semitism that permeated the nineteen-twenties, when the Jew was frequently considered something of a ridiculous comic vaudeville figure, had yielded to the more liberal sentiments of the thirties. Hitler's rise to power and his treatment of the Jews no doubt influenced many writers and thinkers to adopt a more sympathetic attitude toward this group that was suffering such oppression abroad: in 1938, Fitzgerald wrote to his daughter that the Nazis were "obnoxious vermin" and that to share any of their prejudices was a sign of snobbishness and immaturity.

It is impossible to arrive at a perfect understanding of the thoughts and feelings Fitzgerald and Hemingway harbored toward Jews individually or as members of a religious or "racial" group. But this much is clear: in the works of both authors there is a complexity in their treatment of this figure that discourages the application of the term anti-Semite, if by that label we mean an attitude of untempered hostility. In Hemingway's presentation of Robert Cohn there is, to be sure, some condescension; but there is also something like sympathy and understanding. The same ambivalence is paralleled by the characterization of Jews in Fitzgerald's several novels. Perhaps one of the obstructions to a clear understanding here is the term anti-Semitism itself, the definition of which no dictionary can ever adequately supply. But it seems reasonable to say that if Fitzgerald and Hemingway yielded to the popular prejudices of the period, Hemingway did so with only a part of his mind and Fitzgerald did so only momentarily. Robert Cohn is redeemed by his human or sympathetic qualities; Wolfsheim is offset by Bloeckman in *The Beautiful and Damned* and Stahr in *The Last Tycoon*.

A more significant theme that attracted the attention of Fitzgerald and Hemingway, one that occupies considerably more space in their fiction than the alien outsider, is the modern woman. In such works as *The Sun Also Rises, To Have and Have Not, The Fifth Column,* and "The Short Happy Life of Francis Macomber," Hemingway treats this theme; Fitzgerald gives it prominent attention in *The Great Gatsby,* his short story "The Adjuster," and *Tender Is the Night.* Both writers seem essentially in accord in their attitudes toward the particular species of contemporary female they depict in these works; both emphasize her physical attractiveness, her basic egotism, and her destructive influence upon the men with whom she is associated. But before we examine Fitzgerald and Hemingway's treatment of the modern woman, we might find it profitable to consider her appearance in the works of other writers of the period.

Many writers of the nineteen-twenties and early thirties drew portraits of American females who are generally unsympathetic. The women who appear in the stories of Ring Lardner, for example, are almost invariably self-seeking and predatory; occasionally they are stupid and vicious. William Faulkner, too, seems to have contributed to the antifeminism of the time with his depictions of unattractive, calculating, sex-driven daughters of the Southern United States. Sinclair Lewis offered the most extended portrait of the type of American woman who emerged into prominence in the postwar decade. Fran Dodsworth, the wife of Lewis's businessman hero in *Dodsworth,* is a familiar figure to students of the era: selfish, spoiled, adulterous, extravagant, and socially ambitious, she very nearly succeeds in destroying the spirit of her good-humored, trusting mate.

Curiously enough, the most acrid and rancorous treatment of the American female during the nineteen-twenties was done by a European observer. D. H. Lawrence's *Studies in*

Classic American Literature, published in 1922, contains a section of commentary on the character of Pearl, the illegitimate daughter of Hester Prynne in Hawthorne's *Scarlet Letter:*

> Pearl no longer believes in the Divine Father. She says so. She has no Divine Father. Disowns Papa both big and little.
>
> So she can't sin against him.
>
> What will she do then, if she's got no god to sin against? Why, of course, she'll not be able to sin at all. She'll go her own way gaily, and do as she likes, and she'll say, afterwards, when she's made a mess: "Yes, I did it. But I acted for the best, and therefore I am blameless. It's the other person's fault. Or else it's Its fault."

The reader will no doubt feel that he has met Pearl before, or at the very least that she is a strangely prophetic figure. "They were careless people," says Fitzgerald of Daisy and Tom Buchanan in *The Great Gatsby.* "They smashed up things and creatures and then retreated back into their money or their vast carelessness, or whatever it was that kept them together, and let other people clean up the mess. . . ."

But to return to Lawrence and to Pearl:

> She will be blameless, will Pearl, come what may.
>
> And America is a whole rope of these absolutely immaculate Pearls, who can't sin, let them do what they may. Because they've got no god to sin against. Mere men, one after another. Men with no ghost to their name. . . .
>
> By Hawthorne's day it was already Pearl. Before swine, of course. There never yet was a Pearl that wasn't cast before swine.
>
> It's part of her game, part of her pearldom.
>
> Because when Circe lies with a man, *he's* a swine after it, if he wasn't one before. Not *she.* Circe is the great white impeccable Pearl.

Another interruption is in order, and another significant parallel, this time from Hemingway's *The Sun Also Rises.* "Look, Brett," says Mike Campbell in Hemingway's novel. "Tell Jake what Robert calls you. That *is* perfect, you know. . . . He calls her Circe. . . . He claims that she turns men into swine."

And back to Lawrence:

> These dear Pearls, they do anything they like, and remain pure. Oh, purity!
>
> But they can't stop themselves from going rotten inside. Rotten Pearls, fair outside. Their souls smell, because their souls are putrifying inside them.
>
> And gradually, from within outwards, they rot. Some form of dementia. A thing disintegrating. A decomposing psyche. Dementia.

Had Scott Fitzgerald foreseen the tragic destiny of Daisy Buchanan? Years later, when he came to write *Tender Is the Night,* his heroine, Nicole Warren, is diagnosed according to Lawrence's dark prediction: "Diagnostic: Schizophrenie," say the doctors at the psychiatric clinic to which Nicole has been committed: "Phase aigue en decroissance."

If Lawrence's description corresponds imperfectly to the character of Hawthorne's Pearl, it serves admirably as a point of reference, a dramatic statement which represents the views of many authors who left us a vivid image of the American woman under the new "freedom." Earlier, I have attempted a composite portrait of Fitzgerald's young debutante heroine—the beautiful, irresponsible, and narcissistic belle of the intercollegiate dance. In Lardner, in Sinclair Lewis, in the novels and stories of Ernest Hemingway, and in the later works of Fitzgerald himself, there is an agreement of opinion on her older sister—the destructive, egocentric, and domineering woman of the modern epoch. She was

no doubt part of the pattern of social and economic up-
heaval that forms the backdrop for so many themes and
figures who play a part in the literature of the period. She
was the product, too, of the revolution in morals and manners that followed in the wake of peace. She was Fitzgerald's flapper grown up.

Hemingway's first treatment of this character is perhaps
his most famous. Brett Ashley, the Anglo-Saxon counterpart
of the modern American female, is presented for the most
part sympathetically, but is still a member of the class
Lawrence decries. In the scene in which Brett is introduced,
Jake Barnes is drinking at the bar in a Paris dance hall; he
notices that Brett is accompanied by a small crowd of
homosexuals: "With them was Brett. She looked very lovely
and she was very much with them." This is a significant
association; there are similar scenes in Dos Passos' *The
Big Money*, in Lewis's *Dodsworth*, and in Fitzgerald's
Tender Is the Night. The homosexual episodes in each of
these novels suggest the atmosphere of sexual license, excess,
or aberration that characterizes the conduct of the New
Woman. In Hemingway's novel, Brett's mannish clothes
and bobbed hair provide an additional clue to her un-
natural sexuality and her loss of true femininity.[2]

Brett's promiscuity accords with other writers' portrayals
of modern women; it is perhaps the most frequently emphasized aspect of character that they share in common,
the refrain to which they dance through the fiction of the
decade. Brett, it is true, takes moral stock of her own behavior at the end of *The Sun Also Rises;* she decides to
give up her love affair with the bullfighter Pedro Romero.
But earlier Brett's justification of her sexual desire for

[2] See Theodore Bardacke, "Hemingway's Women," reprinted in
Ernest Hemingway: The Man and His Work (New York, 1956), pp.
340-351, for an analysis of Hemingway's attittude toward the postwar
woman.

Romero evokes the familiar strain of self-indulgence typical of Lawrence's Pearl:

> "I'm a goner [says Brett to Jake Barnes]. I'm mad about the Romero boy. I'm in love with him, I think."
> "I wouldn't be if I were you."
> "I can't help it. I'm a goner. It's tearing me all up inside."
> "Don't do it."
> "I can't help it. I've never been able to help anything. . . ."
> "Ask him to come over and have a drink."
> "Not yet. He'll come over."
> "I can't look at him."
> "He's nice to look at," I said.
> "I've always done just what I wanted."
> "I know."
> "I do feel such a bitch."
> "Well," I said.
> "My God!" said Brett, "the things a woman goes through."
> "Yes?"
> "Oh, I do feel such a bitch."

During the late twenties and early thirties Hemingway wrote a number of stories that reveal his attitudes toward the modern woman and the relations between the sexes. Without going into these stories in detail, we might note that Hemingway frequently depicted alienation, perversion, and frustration in his shorter fiction during this period. Fitzgerald seems to have had less interest in the theme of love gone rotten; and his portrayals of modern women, even when unfavorable, are tinged with an archaic gallantry that contrasts sharply with Hemingway's studies of the same subject. Nonetheless, at times, especially in *Tender Is the Night*, Fitzgerald's fictional women bear a remarkable resemblance to the destructive females who appear in Hemingway's novels and stories. These differences and similarities will emerge in some clarity if we juxtapose a few examples from both authors, starting with three of Hemingway's works, written in the middle thirties, that represent a development upon the portrait of the modern woman begun in *The Sun Also Rises*.

In one of these, *To Have and Have Not,* Hemingway gives us a brief description of Dorothy Hollis, the "extraordinarily pretty" wife of a Hollywood motion-picture director. Dorothy is on a pleasure cruise with her lover, a man named Eddie whom Hemingway characterizes as "a professional son-in-law of the very rich." Eddie, it seems, has drunk himself into alcoholic slumber; and Dorothy, who is troubled with insomnia, lies awake in her cabin reflecting on the unpleasant realities of the moment:

> I suppose I'll end up a bitch [she thinks]. Maybe I'm one now. I suppose you never know when you get to be one. Only her best friends would tell her. You don't read it in Mr. Winchell. That would be a good new thing for him to announce. Bitch-hood. Mrs. John Hollis canined into town from the coast. . . . I suppose we all end up as bitches but whose fault is it? The bitches have the most fun but you have to be awfully stupid to be a good one. . . . Stupid and well-intentioned and really selfish to be a good one. Probably I'm one already. They say you can't tell and that you always think you're not. There must be men who don't get tired of you or of it. There must be. But who has them? . . . I wish that luminol would work.

But the luminol fails to work; and Dorothy, fearful of the horrors of a sleepless night, resorts to the grosser sedative of masturbation.

In another work written a few years later, *The Fifth Column,* Hemingway has the hero summarize the general characteristics of his mistress:

> She has the same background all American girls have that come to Europe with a certain amount of money. They're

all the same. Camps, college, money in family, more or less than it was, usually less now, men, affairs, abortions, ambitions, and finally marry and settle down or don't marry and settle down. They open shops, or work in shops, some write, others play instruments, some go on the stage, some into films. They have something called the Junior League I believe that the virgins work at. All for the public good.

Later in the play the hero explains to his girl why he intends to leave her: "You're useless, really. You're uneducated, you're useless, you're a fool and you're lazy." These passages, it is true, represent an extreme and unfortunate manifestation of the Hemingway manner. The easy generalizations, glib rather than authoritative, and the self-conscious virility of the hero's cynicism tend to create the impression of unconscious self-parody. Yet Hemingway's portrait of the "bored Vassar bitch" (as she is called early in the play) is significant as a prominent expression of distaste for the American woman, product of the new dispensation.

But the most important and effective instance of Hemingway's views on this subject is found in his story "The Short Happy Life of Francis Macomber." Written in 1936, "Macomber" contains one of the most memorable—and one of the most merciless—treatments of the American woman in our literature. The story opens as Margot Macomber, wife of the wealthy American-on-safari in Africa, taunts her husband in the presence of Robert Wilson for his cowardice (Francis Macomber has run in terror from a charging lion). "They are the hardest in the world," thinks Wilson, the white hunter and safari guide; "the hardest, the cruelest, the most predatory and the most attractive and their men have softened or gone to pieces nervously as they have hardened. Or is it that they pick men they can handle?" Later Wilson reflects that Margot is "enamelled in that American female cruelty. They are the damnedest women. Really the damnedest." Still later, when Margot is once again calling attention to Macomber's cowardice, Wilson thinks: "She's damn cruel but they're all cruel. They govern, of course, and to govern one has to be cruel sometimes. Still, I've seen enough of their damn terrorism." Hemingway's cynical interpretation of the Macombers' marriage is also relevant as an indication of his attitude toward the American woman: "They had a sound basis of union. Margot was too beautiful for Macomber to divorce her and Macomber had too much money for Margot ever to leave him."

In a central episode in the story Hemingway has Margot Macomber demonstrate her contempt for her husband when she visits the tent of Wilson during the night. When she returns, Macomber, who has been sleepless for several hours, subjects her to a cross-examination in which he pathetically attempts to assert his manhood:

> "Where have you been?" Macomber asked in the darkness.
> "Hello," she said. "Are you awake?"
> "Where have you been?"
> "I just went out to get a breath of air."
> "You did, like hell."
> "What do you want me to say, darling?"
> "Where have you been?"
> "Out to get a breath of air."
> "That's a new name for it. You *are* a bitch."
> "Well, you're a coward."
> "All right," he said. "What of it?"
> "Nothing as far as I'm concerned. But please let's not talk, darling, because I'm very sleepy."
> "You think I'll take anything."
> "I know you will, sweet."

But when Macomber's fear leaves him, as he and the white hunter are stalking buffalo, when he "comes of age," as Wilson calls it, Margot's certainty that her husband will tolerate anything falters. "You know I don't think I'd ever be afraid of anything again," Macomber tells Wilson. "You've gotten awfully brave, awfully suddenly," says Margot; but, Hemingway adds, "her contempt was not secure." She is afraid, presumably, that her husband will leave her. Desperate at the thought of losing her mastery over the man, she shoots him as he and Wilson attempt to stop the advance of a wounded buffalo. Wilson has the final word: "That was a pretty thing to do," he tells her. "He *would* have left you too."

Margot Macomber is in no sense typical of Hemingway's fictional women. Obviously she is an extreme representative of the class of female characters I am describing here. Yet she possesses those qualities of character (in exaggerated form perhaps) which Hemingway and other writers of the period consistently emphasized in their depictions of the modern woman. She is aggressive, domineering, sexually indulgent (either promiscuous, adulterous, or in some way aberrant), idle, and egocentric.

Fitzgerald's later heroines, at least in a few outstanding instances, are remarkably similar in conduct and character. I have already commented in some detail upon Fitzgerald's portrayal of Daisy Buchanan and Jordan Baker of *The Great Gatsby*, both of whom share many traits in common with Hemingway's unsavory females. Jordan's masculine aggressiveness, her dishonesty, her selfishness and narcissism tend to support this contention. Daisy, too, qualifies for admission to the sisterhood: she is basically insincere; she indulges in an adulterous liaison with Jay Gatsby, she is devoted to the pursuit of hedonistic and expensive pleasures; and most important, she ignores her share of responsibility in the death of Myrtle Wilson, by which action she contributes to the murder of her lover. In Daisy Buchanan and Jordan

Baker, Fitzgerald seems to be implying that the modern American woman is not only deficient in character (to use an unfashionable epithet) and incapable of love, but also that she might be dangerous to encounter on any but the most casual basis.

Another of Fitzgerald's spoiled heroines is Luella Hemple of "The Adjuster," published the same year as *The Great Gatsby*. Early in this story Fitzgerald emphasizes the position of Luella and her husband as members of a generation cut adrift from the values of the immediate past:

> They were of that enormous American class who wander over Europe every summer, sneering rather pathetically and wistfully at the customs and traditions and pastimes of other countries, because they have no customs or tradition or pastimes of their own. It is a class sprung yesterday from fathers and mothers who might just as well have lived two hundred years ago.

This modern rootlessness has unfortunate consequences in the case of Luella and Charles Hemple. Luella's freedom from the household duties that were a necessary condition of the wives of an earlier era leaves her "wanting something to do." "Even my baby bores me," Luella confides to a friend. "He doesn't *begin* to fill my life." And later Luella protests to Doctor Moon, a stranger whom Charles Hemple has brought home to dinner:

> "Don't you see I've had enough of home?" Her breasts seemed to struggle for air under her dress. "Don't you see how bored I am with keeping house, with the baby—everything seems as if it's going on forever and ever? I want excitement; and I don't care what form it takes or what I pay for it, so long as it makes my heart beat." . . .
>
> "I've tried to be good, and I'm not going to try any more. If I'm one of those women who wreck their lives for nothing, then I'll do it now. You can call me selfish, or silly, and be

quite right; but in five minutes I'm going out of this house and begin to be alive."

For Charles Hemple, the strain of supporting all the responsibilities of the household proves too great. He suffers a nervous breakdown on the very night Luella has decided to leave him in pursuit of "excitement."

> Charles Hemple had had a nervous collapse. . . . His attitude toward his wife was the weak point in what had otherwise been a strong-minded and well-organized career—he was aware of her intense selfishness, but it is one of the many flaws in the scheme of human relationships that selfishness in women has an irresistible appeal to many men. Luella's selfishness existed side by side with a childish beauty, and in consequence, Charles Hemple had begun to take the blame upon himself for situations which she had obviously brought about. It was an unhealthy attitude, and his mind had sickened. . . .

Charles Hemple's illness affects Luella in two ways: it makes her reconsider her decision to leave him and it adds another task to the domestic obligations she already loathes: "The question of her liberties had to be postponed until he was on his feet. Just when she had determined to be a wife no longer, Luella was compelled to be a nurse as well." But faced with these new difficulties, Luella begins to adopt a different attitude: "I do what I have to do—" she tells Doctor Moon, who has become a regular visitor at the Hemple residence and whom Luella has come to regard as a confidant. Later, when Luella's child dies, she accepts the loss; and at Doctor Moon's insistence, she devotes herself more and more unselfishly to helping her husband recover.

Near the end of the story Fitzgerald reveals that Doctor Moon is a personification of the passage of time. "We make an agreement with children that they can sit in the audience without helping to make the play," he tells Luella, "but if they still sit in the audience after they're grown, somebody's got to work double time for them, so that they can enjoy the light and glitter of the world."

> "It's your turn to be the centre, to give others what was given to you for so long. You've got to give security to young people and peace to your husband, and a sort of charity to the old. You've got to let the people who work for you depend on you. You've got to cover up a few more troubles than you show, and be a little more patient than the average person, and do a little more instead of a little less than your share. The light and glitter of the world is in your hands."

The conclusion of "The Adjuster" reveals Luella Hemple with a "mature kindness about her face at twenty-eight [apparently, for Fitzgerald, the threshold of middle-age!], as if suffering had touched her only reluctantly and then hurried away." Charles Hemple has completely recovered; Luella has matured through suffering; and she has become a devoted mother to two children Fitzgerald introduces, as a crowning implausibility, in the last sentence.[3]

"The Adjuster" is typical of Fitzgerald's popular-magazine fiction in its tone of mild reproach for Luella's attitudes, its avoidance of the theme of sexual license (though Luella's craving for "excitement" suggests the possibility), and in its optimistic and unconvincing conclusion. Hemingway's portrayals of the destructive modern woman are, of course, more cynical and more realistic than this. Yet there is a parallel between the two authors' treatments of this subject worth noticing. Hemingway's Brett Ashley and Fitzgerald's

[3] Cf. Fitzgerald's story "The Lees of Happiness," which also emphasizes the theme of maturity through suffering.

Luella Hemple both represent partially sympathetic depictions of the postwar woman.

In later works both writers grow increasingly disillusioned with the possibility of her attaining wisdom, maturity, or the capacity to love. Margot Macomber is the logical successor to Brett Ashley; and Nicole and Baby Warren, of *Tender Is the Night*, are the successors to Luella Hemple. Pedro Romero, the bullfighter whom Brett renounces in *The Sun Also Rises*, must be counted a fortunate survivor in the modern battle of the sexes. Likewise Charles Hemple of "The Adjuster." Both have escaped the fate of their later counterparts, Francis Macomber and Dick Diver.

The actual passage of years apparently subverted Fitzgerald's faith in Doctor Moon.

In *Tender Is the Night* the defeat of the sentimental American male is no longer potential but real. The fascination Fitzgerald's heroes have with physical beauty captivates Dick Diver (as it captivates Francis Macomber): "Her face, ivory gold against the blurred sunset that strove through the rain, had a promise Dick had never seen before: the high cheek-bones, the faintly wan quality, cool rather than feverish, was reminiscent of the frame of a promising colt—a creature whose life did not promise to be only a projection of youth upon a grayer screen, but instead, a true growing; the face would be handsome in middle life; it would be handsome in old age: the essential structure and economy were there."

The potency of Nicole Warren's appeal is given emphasis by Diver's decision to marry her; for he knows that marriage to Nicole is inadvisable. She is mentally unstable, a schizophrenic recently discharged from a clinic in Zurich; and Baby Warren, Nicole's sister, looks upon Diver as a useful psychiatric caretaker, rather than a husband to Nicole.

Diver's resentment of Baby's attitude yields, however, to Nicole's fatal attractiveness:

> "*Big* chance—oh, yes [Diver reflects]. My God!—they decided to buy a doctor? Well, they better stick to whoever they've got in Chicago." Revolted by his harshness he made amends to Nicole, remembering that nothing had ever felt so young as her lips, remembering rain like tears shed for him that lay upon her softly shining porcelain cheeks . . . the silence of the storm ceasing woke him about three o'clock and he went to the window. Her beauty climbed the rolling slope, it came into the room, rustling ghost-like through the curtains. . . .

The process by which Diver gradually loses his own emotional sturdiness, his capacity to love, and his ambition constitutes the heart of Fitzgerald's novel. As Nicole slowly recovers her sanity, attended through crisis after crisis by Diver's affectionate care, her character reasserts itself: "Moment by moment all that Dick had taught her fell away and she was nearer to what she had been at the beginning," says Fitzgerald of his heroine near the end of the novel. "Being well perhaps I've gone back to my true self," admits Nicole a few pages earlier. And: "other women have lovers," she muses; "why not me?"

Not long after Nicole commences her love affair with the handsome adventurer Tommy Barban, Diver leaves for America; by this time he has become something of an alcoholic and a social nuisance: he has served his purpose. "Dick was a good husband to me for six years," Nicole tells Baby Warren. "All that time I never suffered a minute's pain because of him, and he always did his best never to let anything hurt me." To which Baby replies: "That's what he was educated for." The final impression Fitzgerald gives us of his hero is that he is practicing medicine "in one town or another" of the Finger Lakes section—"a pleasant place" in New York state. The pattern Fitzgerald traces in *Tender Is the Night* parallels the statement made by Wilson, the white hunter of Hemingway's "The Short Happy Life of Francis Macomber": "They are the hardest in the world; the hardest, the cruelest, the most predatory and the most attractive and their men have softened or gone to pieces nervously as they have hardened."

Fitzgerald's treatment of the Dick Diver-Nicole Warren relationship, however, is characteristically more romantic than anything comparable in the works of Ernest Hemingway. Indeed, the history of Dick Diver is reminiscent of one of the central and typical myths of nineteenth-century Romanticism—a theme which finds its most celebrated expression in Keats's "La Belle Dame Sans Merci." Like the abandoned hero of Keats's poem, Diver is incapable of heeding the whispered warning: "La Belle Dame sans Merci/Hath thee in thrall." The penalty is spiritual desolation:

> O what can ail thee, knight-at-arms,
>   Alone and palely loitering?
> The sedge has withered from the lake
>   And no birds sing.

In *Tender Is the Night* Fitzgerald has transmuted into modern terms the Romantic image of the bewitched innocent, victimized by the fairy temptress.

Yet there are pages in Fitzgerald's novel that approach the more realistic manner of Hemingway's "Short Happy Life of Francis Macomber," as when Baby Warren is urging a reluctant American consul to rush to the assistance of Dick Diver:

> "You put on your hat and come with me right away" [insists Baby].

The mention of his hat alarmed the Consul who began to clean his spectacles hurriedly and to ruffle his papers. This proved to no avail: the American Woman, aroused, stood over him; the clean-sweeping irrational temper that had broken the moral back of a race and made a nursery out of a continent, was too much for him. He rang for the vice-consul—Baby had won.

And if Nicole does not literally blow off the back of her mate's head, she does assist in the gradual destruction of his will. At one point, indeed, Fitzgerald suggests that she figuratively devours him:

"Kiss me, on the lips, Tommy" [Nicole says].
"That's so American," he said, kissing her nevertheless. "When I was in America last there were girls who would tear you apart with their lips, tear themselves too, until their faces were scarlet with the blood around the lips all brought out in a patch. . . ."

At the same time, Nicole is more complicated in her motives and attitudes than Margot Macomber, perhaps more recognizable as an American type than Hemingway's extreme of spite, malice, and selfishness. Notwithstanding these differences in tone and emphasis, the modern women portrayed by Hemingway and Fitzgerald share in common a number of characteristics; and they seem to exercise a similar influence upon their unfortunate mates. Dispensers of woe, the females in the American fiction of the nineteen-twenties leave behind them men embittered, shattered, or dead.

Closely related to the depiction of the modern woman in Hemingway and Fitzgerald is the interest both writers displayed in the theme of the ruined writer. Fitzgerald's *Tender Is the Night* and Hemingway's "The Snows of Kilimanjaro," which were published within a two-year period, are two of the most effective treatments of this theme in American literature. Furthermore, these two works not only stress the same theme, but develop as well similar plots and characters.

The destroyed writer is an American phenomenon and something of an American preoccupation. The fate of such literary artists as Edgar Allan Poe and Hart Crane seems more typical, to many observers at least, than the opposite image of established solidity typified by William Dean Howells. Van Wyck Brooks, for example, has commented at some length upon what he calls "the abortive career" of the American literary artist. The same theme has attracted the attention of some of our leading fictionists: Henry James remarked that the American writer seemed destined to follow a pattern of "broken careers, orphaned children, early disasters, violent deaths." James's comment is but one of many that stress the native tendency toward unfulfilled talent, alcoholism, and suicide—comments that seem to culminate in Fitzgerald's "Crack-Up" essays. "No one of us escapes it," said Sherwood Anderson, speaking of the "tragedy" of the creative man in America. "How can he?"

If Anderson's remark is exaggerated, it is nevertheless true that many American writers, among them Ring Lardner and Scott Fitzgerald, reveal a tendency toward tragic misfortune in their personal and professional histories. It is also true that the theme of the ruined writer has received considerable attention from many of our critics and fictionists. Hemingway appears to have been much interested in this theme in the mid nineteen-thirties, but his fullest and most important treatment of it occurs in "The Snows of Kilimanjaro" (written in 1936). The hero of the story, a man named Harry, has for a number of years entertained a profound desire to write about his experiences, vividly remembered from his wanderings in Europe and America.

But he has never realized this ambition; instead, he has gradually yielded to his preference for the pleasures of love-making, the company of rich women, and the life of ease that has softened his determination to exercise his literary talent. It is Harry's failure, treated in a tone of overwhelming regret, that Hemingway dramatizes in "The Snows of Kilimanjaro."

The story is set in Africa, where Harry and his wealthy American wife have set out upon a hunting expedition; Harry has the idea that the rigors of the trip will help toughen him up and restore his creative powers, or at least restore his ability to apply himself to his work. But the safari breaks down when one of the native guides burns out a bearing in the truck and Harry discovers that a cut on his leg has become infected and gangrenous. Now, as he lies dying of his wound—a symbol of the decay of his talent—Harry relives in his mind those experiences he has wanted to record on paper. He also tries to define the reasons for his failure to do so.

> Now he would never write the things that he had saved to write until he knew enough to write them well. Well, he would not have to fail at trying to write them either. Maybe you could never write them, and that was why you put them off and delayed the starting. Well he would never know, now.
>
> What was his talent anyway? It was a talent all right but instead of using it, he had traded on it. It was never what he had done, but always what he could do. And he had chosen to make his living with something else instead of a pen or a pencil.
>
> We must all be cut out for what we do, he thought. However you make your living is where your talent lies. He had sold vitality, in one form or another, all his life and when your affections are not too involved you give much better value for the money. He had found that out

but he would never write that, now, either. No, he would
not write that, although it was well worth writing.

She shot very well this good, this rich bitch, this kindly
caretaker and destroyer of his talent. Nonsense. He had
destroyed his talent himself. Why should he blame this
woman because she kept him well? He had destroyed his
talent by not using it, by betrayals of himself and what he
believed in, by drinking so much that he blunted the edge
of his perceptions, by laziness, by sloth, and by snobbery,
by pride and by prejudice, by hook and by crook.

If Harry's tragedy sounds somehow familiar to readers
of the fiction of the period, it is because Scott Fitzgerald
had rehearsed the same story a few years earlier in *Tender
Is the Night*. Dick Diver, too, has "sold vitality, in one
form or another"—to the group of expatriates who are drawn
to his control and charm, and to his wife Nicole, whom he
has been "hired" to love and protect. Like Harry, Diver
has undergone emotional and professional deterioration
because his wife's wealth has made effort unnecessary; like
Hemingway's hero, Dick Diver has become accustomed
to the comfort that corrupts the will and destroys ambition.
Like Harry, too, Diver is ambivalent about the reasons for
his deterioration: he vacillates between placing the blame
upon his own weakness and the seductive leisure purchased
by the Warren fortune: "I can't do anything for you any
more," says Diver to Nicole near the end of the novel. "I'm
trying to save myself."

> "From my contamination?" [asks Nicole.]
> "Profession throws me in contact with questionable com-
> pany sometimes."
> She wept with anger at the abuse.
> "You're a coward! You've made a failure of your life, and
> you want to blame it on me."

Diver and Harry also share similar attitudes, in their

decline, toward the wealthy class of American idlers with whom they have been associated. "The rich were dull and they drank too much," Harry reflects near the end of Hemingway's story. "They were dull and they were repetitious." In one of the concluding chapters of Fitzgerald's novel, Mary Minghetti tells Dick Diver: "Nobody cares whether you drink or not. Even when Abe drank hardest, he never offended people like you do." Diver replies: "You're all so dull."

Finally, for all the surface description of Diver's professional involvements with psychiatry, the hero of *Tender Is the Night* may be accurately considered a ruined artist of the sort Hemingway writes about in "The Snows of Kilimanjaro." By making his hero a doctor rather than a writer Fitzgerald no doubt hoped to gain distance and detachment. But his efforts were not completely successful. Biographical data support the notion, already mentioned by several students of Fitzgerald's fiction, that in *Tender Is the Night* the novelist was projecting his anxiety about his own career and emotional instability.[4] There is, furthermore, strong internal evidence that Fitzgerald conceived of Dick Diver's career as parallel, in many respects, to his own. All through *Tender Is the Night* there are references to Diver's literary activity. An early episode mentions his publication of an extremely popular medical treatise ("The little book is selling everywhere," says Nicole. "They want it published in six languages.")—an obvious counterpart to Fitzgerald's best-selling novels. And during the central sections of *Tender Is the Night* Diver struggles, at times aimlessly, to complete another medical text. Finally, in the last chapter Fitzgerald returns to the unfinished manuscript to give particular emphasis to Diver's loss of ambition, the

[4] See, for example, Arthur Mizener, *The Far Side of Paradise* (Cambridge, Mass., 1951), pp. 245-251.

decline of his professional dedication: "he always had a big stack of papers on his desk that were known to be an important treatise on some medical subject, almost in process of completion."[5]

Thus Fitzgerald's *Tender Is the Night* traces the same pattern as "The Snows of Kilimanjaro" and reveals, indirectly at least, the same interest in the blighted artistic career and the decay of a writer's talent. An important aspect of Diver's tragedy, like Harry's, is that "he would never write the things he had saved to write until he knew enough to write them well." It might also be worth repeating, in conclusion, that Harry and Dick Diver have been victimized by the same forces. Temperamental weakness, to be sure, plays a part in the misfortunes of both heroes. But Hemingway and Fitzgerald have stressed as well the ruinous influence of a luxurious life provided by wealthy American women.

We might conclude, on the basis of the foregoing comparative readings, that the conception of Fitzgerald as an author who glamorized the rich is true only in a limited sense; and that Fitzgerald and Hemingway, for all their obvious differences, were basically in agreement upon many features of contemporary experience. There is of course a great deal of evidence which demonstrates the attraction Fitzgerald felt, and Hemingway did not feel, for wealth and the way of life it could purchase. The opening of *Tender Is the Night,* the company of idle expatriates held together by the charm of Dick and Nicole Diver, the glittering appeal of the debutante Daisy Fay in *The Great Gatsby,* and

[5] For the idea that Diver might be considered a professional writer, rather than a doctor, I am indebted to the unpublished dissertation (University of Pennsylvania, 1950) by Henry Dan Piper, "Scott Fitzgerald and the Origins of the Jazz Age," pp. 132-134.

the parties given at Gatsby's mansion—these episodes in the life of the American rich Fitzgerald invests with a kind of glamor and excitement. But Fitzgerald can not be said to have glamorized Tom Buchanan; nor did the author of *Gatsby* leave any doubt, at the conclusion of the novel, about the insincerity and corruption of Daisy. It is also very difficult to mistake Fitzgerald's view of the wealthy class personified by the Warren family in *Tender Is the Night*. Baby Warren in particular is as unappealing a character as any of the rich American women who appear in the works of Hemingway and Sinclair Lewis during the same period. Nicole Warren, it is true, is initially portrayed as attractive and sympathetic; but this impression fades as she recovers from her mental illness. Fitzgerald suggests that Dick Diver, the sentimental knight-at-arms in a strange land, finds Nicole fascinating for her youth and beauty and for her helpless dependency; but, as we have seen, these are not the qualities of the real Nicole Warren. Diver has merely loved her for a time when she was not herself.

On the other hand, much of the texture of Fitzgerald's novels and stories—the descriptions of dinners and motor trips and parties and conversations—evokes an image of leisure-class charm and alluring opulence. In Hemingway such an emphasis is almost completely absent. Had Fitzgerald written "The Snows of Kilimanjaro" (a speculation not without relevance here), the content of Harry's dying thoughts would have consisted of the social activities in which he and Helen had participated, rather than the episodes of sexual pleasure and violent action that Harry remembers. A great deal of Fitzgerald's interest *was* in the Ritz and in playboys, as Christian Gauss observed; and if the novelist's characteristic fable was a modern interpre-

tation of "La Belle Dame Sans Merci," it is undeniable that
the song of the demon temptress was a lyrical celebration of
money.

Yet the affinities in the works of Scott Fitzgerald and
Ernest Hemingway are as important as the differences.
Their treatments of the themes of the alien outsider, the
modern woman, and the ruined writer reflect similar attitudes; and with particular reference to the last of these,
Hemingway and Fitzgerald seem to be in complete accord
on the disaster latent in one aspect of the American Dream.

III

Fitzgerald's influence on Hemingway is difficult to define and must be based on the always inconclusive evidence
of parallels. A number of critics have already called attention to several of these parallels. Oscar Cargill thought the
story "Out of Season" reflected the manner of Scott Fitzgerald, as did the opening pages of *The Sun Also Rises*.
More recently Philip Young has remarked that several
Hemingway stories which portray disillusioned or corrupted
love affairs were derived from Fitzgerald's treatments of the
same theme or mood.

Critics have overlooked the strong resemblance between
Tender Is the Night and Hemingway's African stories.
Both "The Short Happy Life of Francis Macomber" and
"The Snows of Kilimanjaro," it seems to me, were drawn
from Fitzgerald's novel, which Hemingway read two years
before he wrote these stories. The situation and development of the characters in "Macomber" seem particularly
reminiscent of Dick Diver and Nicole and Baby Warren.
Hemingway has made an important modification: in *Tender
Is the Night* the hero's strength declines as his wife's in-
creases; in "Macomber" the hero acquires strength as his
wife declines into relative weakness. Hemingway has re-

versed Fitzgerald's pattern of the transfer of power; but
the basic pattern is still clearly discernible. "Kilimanjaro,"
on the other hand, adheres closely to Fitzgerald's conception of the disintegration of character in *Tender Is the
Night*. The causes of the hero's misfortunes, furthermore,
show a close correspondence in Hemingway's story and
Fitzgerald's novel. Perhaps Hemingway's adoption of these
ideas was unconscious; but it is certain that Fitzgerald's
novel left a strong impression on his friend's imagination.
A year after *Tender Is the Night* was published Hemingway wrote Maxwell Perkins: "A strange thing is that in
retrospect his Tender Is the Night gets better and better."

Hemingway's influence on Fitzgerald is most clearly
apparent in the style of *Tender Is the Night*. It is true that
Fitzgerald's mature style was shaped in part by his experience over the years: he had traveled widely during the
period 1925-1934; he had had close associations with a
number of writers; his personal difficulties might well have
tempered the extravagance of his imagination; and the
nation had undergone a sobering psychological adjustment
to the hardships of the new decade. These circumstances
may have diminished Fitzgerald's intense and colorful poetic
invention and may have inclined him toward more realistic
reflection, with a heightened emphasis on verisimilitude.
Whatever the reasons, by the early thirties the tone of poetic
fantasy in *The Great Gatsby* had evolved into the more
concrete solidity of *Tender Is the Night*.

The distinguishing quality of the later novel is founded
in part on its language. *Tender Is the Night* still retains the
clarity of diction, the measured cadence, and the evocative
imagery that have impressed readers of *Gatsby*:

> They reached the hotel and Rosemary walked a little
> behind him, to admire him, to adore him. His step was
> alert as if he had just come from some great doings and

was hurrying on toward others. Organizer of private gaiety, curator of a richly incrusted happiness. His hat was a perfect hat and he carried a heavy stick and yellow gloves. . . .

They walked upstairs—five flights. At the first landing they stopped and kissed; she was careful on the next landing, on the third more careful still. On the next—there were two more—she stopped half way and kissed him fleetingly good-by. At his urgency she walked down with him to the one below for a minute—and then up and up. Finally it was good-by with their hands stretching to touch along the diagonal of the banister and then the fingers slipping apart.

But in Fitzgerald's mature style there is nothing so airy and fanciful as the following passage from *The Great Gatsby:*

One autumn night, five years before, they had been walking down the street when the leaves were falling, and they came to a place where there were no trees and the sidewalk was white with moonlight. They stopped here and turned toward each other. Now it was a cool night with that mysterious excitement in it which comes at the two changes of the year. The quiet lights in the houses were humming out into the darkness and there was a stir and bustle among the stars. Out of the corner of his eye Gatsby saw that the blocks of the sidewalks really formed a ladder and mounted to a secret place above the trees— he could climb to it, if he climbed alone, and once there he could suck on the pap of life, gulp down the incomparable milk of wonder.

We know that Fitzgerald read *A Farewell to Arms* while he was writing *Tender Is the Night,* and that in the late twenties he also gave some of Hemingway's short stories careful perusal. Hemingway's imagery, spare and conservative but invested with a unique and powerful poetic effect, established a claim on Fitzgerald's susceptible imagination, so much so that he felt it advisable to stop reading

Hemingway during this period, lest the latter's "rhythms" begin to creep into his own sentences. In addition, Hemingway may have stated, in conversation with Fitzgerald, his feelings about inflated prose—which he expressed at some length in *Death in the Afternoon,* written in 1930 and 1931. There are many writers, remarked Hemingway, who inject a fake mystical quality into their prose in order to disguise their inability to state clearly. Other writers afflicted with the same necessity praise such work in self-defense. But overwritten journalism elevated by a false epic tone is not literature, etc. Hemingway's implication here is that clear and realistic writing is one of the ultimate values for the prose artist. And though there is nothing of the fake epic quality about *The Great Gatsby,* there is an elevated and heightened poetic tone. Fitzgerald might well have taken to heart Hemingway's comments on the ability to state clearly, thereby effecting the modification of his style which is evident in *Tender Is the Night.*

In addition to the quality of language and imagery, *Tender Is the Night* emphasizes more than any of Fitzgerald's earlier works what Hemingway called "the way it was"—a concept, as Carlos Baker has pointed out, that was one of the basic tenets of Hemingway's aesthetic. Professor Baker believes that this artistic principle is the foundation of Hemingway's consistent evocation of a sense of place, a sense of fact, and a sense of scene.[6] Fitzgerald's first novel, *This Side of Paradise,* certainly emphasizes all of these; yet *This Side of Paradise* is rather special in that it attempts to dramatize place, fact, and scene more than it does action, character, or idea: "the way it was" constitutes its core and primary significance. *The Great Gatsby,* too, dramatically evokes a sense of place by its skillful representation of the *feeling* of New York City; but here,

[6] *Hemingway,* pp. 48-54.

as elsewhere in the novel, Fitzgerald's mode of expression
is poetic and fanciful:

> Over the great bridge, with the sunlight through the girders
> making a constant flicker upon the moving cars, with the
> city rising up across the river in white heaps and sugar
> lumps all built with a wish out of non-olfactory money. The
> city seen from the Queensboro Bridge is always the city
> seen for the first time, in its wild promise of all the mystery
> and beauty in the world.

Fitzgerald's mode in *Tender Is the Night* is more deliberately realistic and discursive. The sense of place is
pervasive and vivid: the opening section, in which Fitzgerald establishes Gausse's Hotel beach as the setting for
the drama between Rosemary Hoyt and the Divers, might
be mentioned as one memorable instance. Others could
easily be added—such as the visit to the battlefield in Chapter XIII of Book One; or the description of Zurich and
Dohmler's clinic in Chapter II, Book Two; or the party on
board T. F. Golding's yacht in Chapter V, Book Three.
The sense of fact, too, is stronger in *Tender Is the Night*
than elsewhere in Fitzgerald's fiction; the novelist appears
to have taken more than usual care with specific dates
and locations, and Dick Diver's involvement with psychiatry
compelled the use of data to an extent that was not required
in Fitzgerald's earlier novels.

But an even more prominent aspect of *Tender Is the
Night* is its sense of scene, its consistent excellence in
conjuring up in the reader's mind a dramatic situation that
takes place in a particularly appropriate setting. One of the
most perfectly realized of these scenes occurs early in
Book Two, when Dick Diver and Nicole Warren meet in
a hidden spot on the grounds of the clinic and listen to
Nicole's phonograph as it plays the popular American songs
of the day:

They were in America now, even Franz with his conception of Dick as an irresistible Lothario would never have guessed that they had gone so far away. They were sorry, dear; they went down to meet each other in a taxi, honey; they had preferences in smiles and had met in Hindustan; and shortly afterward they must have quarreled, for nobody knew and nobody seemed to care—yet finally one of them had gone and left the other crying, only to feel blue, to feel sad.

The thin tunes, holding lost times and future hopes in liaison, twisted upon the Valais night. In the lulls of the phonograph a cricket held the scene together with a single note. By and by Nicole stopped playing the machine and sang to him.

Fitzgerald provides an abundance of episodes such as this one, in which character, setting, and action become fused in a single vivid pictorial image. Another instance may be found near the end of the novel when Nicole and Dick Diver sit with Tommy Barban at a café table and decide the fate of their marriage. Or shortly thereafter, when Fitzgerald constructs the astonishing tableau of Dick's farewell gesture:

As he stood up, he swayed a little; he did not feel well any more—his blood raced slow. He raised his hand and with a papal cross he blessed the beach from the high terrace. Faces turned upward from several umbrellas.

Thus with many other scenes and episodes in the novel, all rendered with a richness of verisimilitude not found in Fitzgerald's earlier work.

In its technique, then—in its concrete rather than fanciful language, and in its realistic evocation of place, fact, and scene—Fitzgerald's *Tender Is the Night* approaches the spirit and manner of the art of Ernest Hemingway. This is not to say that the novel reads like anything written by

Hemingway; but it does reflect a modification in Fitzgerald's perspective on the craft of fiction. The evidence I have set forth here, both biographical and textual, strongly suggests that that modification was a result of Fitzgerald's admiration for his friend and colleague.

With the recent death of Ernest Hemingway and the promised release, some time in the future, of his volume of reminiscences about the nineteen-twenties, more light on his relationship with Scott Fitzgerald will no doubt be forthcoming. In the meantime the general pattern and important particulars are clear: Fitzgerald and Hemingway were close companions, strong personalities who for a time affected the course of each other's lives; they turned their thoughts and their talents on occasion toward the same themes and subjects and left us enduring interpretations of the same features of national experience; and each author exerted a significant influence on the other's fiction.

It is enough—and not enough. Notebooks, correspondence, literary parallels and allusions—these touch only the surface of the deeper story; let the reader himself supply the content between the lines, beneath and behind the lines. The most diligent of historians can never re-create the lavish expenditure of intellect and emotion—true component of all our friendships.

CHAPTER VI

Perspectives

> "I am more of a solitary than I have ever been. . . ." —FITZGERALD TO HIS DAUGHTER

Fitzgerald wrote in 1932 that he had once believed there were no second acts in American lives. Fitzgerald admirers have adopted this observation as a pet epigram and have made it part of the celebrated legend. But it is curiously inappropriate to the American life represented by Fitzgerald himself. There was of course the gaudy but appealing first act with its drama of youth and success. With the beautiful Zelda at his side Fitzgerald dominated the stage with an intensity which suggested, perhaps even to himself, that the episodes to follow would be inevitably anticlimactic. Yet the years of disillusion and decline, in the late twenties and early thirties, have a vivid interest of their own; and they were succeeded by what Malcolm Cowley has called a "third act and epilogue"—a period as important for an understanding of Scott Fitzgerald as anything that came before.

Most of this last period was spent in Hollywood during the years 1937-1940. Here Fitzgerald was occupied with a number of odd jobs writing for the studios and with the composition of approximately thirty short stories (most of which appeared in *Esquire*). He also engaged in a deeply felt, though erratic, love affair and suffered a series of lapses into alcoholism and ill-health. And near the end he applied himself to serious literary work on his Hollywood novel, *The Last Tycoon*. Underlying all this activity we may discern a consistent extension of the pattern I have traced throughout this study: the impulse on Fitzgerald's part toward finding a new source of influence and inspiration, the temperamental urge to discover someone to respect and emulate, someone who might impart new ideas and kindle the imagination to new creative efforts.

A brief review of Fitzgerald's professional development up to this point will help us establish the significance of the Hollywood years. A true development it was, unmistakably: each of Fitzgerald's four novels represented a change of approach to the materials of fiction and the treatment of those materials. His style underwent a transformation from novel to novel: the episodic, poetic, and dramatic *This Side of Paradise* was succeeded by the more consistently narrative *Beautiful and Damned; The Great Gatsby* exhibited skillful selection and organization; *Tender Is the Night* revealed increased powers of mature and realistic observation. Fitzgerald's ideas and themes, too, show a process of expansion and increasing depth over the years. His first novel—with its emphasis on the personality of the hero, its fabric of undergraduate days, young love, and exuberant, half-formulated theories of life and society—suggests the author's youth and intellectual naïveté. *The Beautiful and Damned* reflects Fitzgerald's awareness of wider areas of American behavior and American society, while *The*

Great Gatsby reveals the novelist in the act of judging (rather than simply exploring) the values of a particular social class. *Tender Is the Night* conveys Fitzgerald's mature impressions of the American leisure class and the disaster latent in the American Dream; it exhibits these themes on a broader canvas than *Gatsby;* it shows familiarity with a European setting; and it comprehends a larger and more diverse dramatis personae. In both style and content Fitzgerald's novels trace a course of continuous growth, a dynamic contour embracing variety, change, and increased understanding.

I have tried to show in earlier chapters how closely Fitzgerald's professional development was related to his personal associations with other writers. Here, too, there was a course of change and variety. In his most active and productive years Fitzgerald seemed to leap from enthusiasm to enthusiasm: "You are the best guide, the best judge of my work" is a consistent refrain from his days at Princeton to the publication of *Tender Is the Night;* and we recall that he applied this phrase (or words to the same effect) to Wilson, Mencken, and Hemingway successively. These personal enthusiasms, it seems clear, were reflected in the matter and manner of Fitzgerald's fiction. Edmund Wilson played a part in the composition of Fitzgerald's first three novels; Mencken influenced *The Beautiful and Damned* and *The Vegetable;* Lardner contributed important elements to *The Great Gatsby;* and Hemingway left an indelible impression on "The Rich Boy" and *Tender Is the Night*. Fitzgerald's casual admission, in 1920, that he was "a professed literary thief, hot after the best methods of every writer in my generation" [1] is a significant bit of

---

[1] "An interview with F. Scott Fitzgerald," *Saturday Review*, XLIII:45 (Nov. 5, 1960), 56. Originally written in 1920, but not published until 1960.

self-awareness; but his instinct for such pilfering was to develop into something more. He was to test his ideas against some of the best minds of his time, to absorb their impressions and deepen his own understanding of his craft, and to profit enormously from their insights and experience.

It might be presumptuous to claim that Fitzgerald was dependent—perhaps more so than was good for him personally—on the stimulation provided by other writers. Yet there are occasional passages in his works that support this notion. The Richard Caramel motif in *The Beautiful and Damned* is a revealing instance of Fitzgerald's thoughts on the subject: Caramel, the shallow but extremely successful writer who makes infrequent appearances in the novel, confesses at one point that he is writing faster, and thinking less, since his intellectual companions have ceased to provide him with conversation and stimulation. Years later Fitzgerald recorded in "The Crack-Up" series his own frightened realization that the years of dependency had resulted in disorientation and a fragmented personality:

> For twenty years a certain man had been my intellectual conscience. That was Edmund Wilson. . . . Another man represented my sense of the "good life". . . . A third contemporary had been an artistic conscience to me. . . . A fourth man had come to dictate my relations with other people. . . . So there was not an "I" any more—not a basis on which I could organize my self-respect. . . . It was strange to have no self—to be like a little boy left alone in a big house, who knew that he could do anything he wanted to do, but found that there was nothing that he wanted to do—

In the same series of essays Fitzgerald listed all writers as among the people he found intolerable: "I avoided writers very carefully because they can perpetuate trouble as no one else can."

What "trouble" was he thinking of? Snubs from Wilson?

Bad reviews from Mencken? Quarrels with Hemingway? Or was it a more general trouble—a sense that he had given himself emotionally, and leaned on others intellectually, without a thought to conserving his inner resources or, finally, his identity? In any case, he was now a little boy in a big house with nothing to do—a feeling that must have been intensified by the fact that there was no Wilson or Mencken or Lardner or Hemingway on his horizon. Doubtless he was in no mood to initiate another such companionship, with its concomitant burden of admiration, study, and struggle for self-enrichment: his mounting debts, his wife's illness, his own poor health, and his professional inertia—the middle nineteen-thirties were Fitzgerald's years of disappointment and despair, his "dark night of the soul." The effort required to summon the old enthusiasm was not to be thought of; and then, even if he had been willing, could anyone within his diminishing circle of acquaintances qualify as a new guide and judge? Fitzgerald's prospects at this time seemed desperately slim and unpromising.

Yet "The Crack-Up," which recorded these depressing circumstances with ruthless cynicism, represented the first step on the road back. Arnold Gingrich remembers visiting Fitzgerald, late in 1935, to urge him to submit material to *Esquire*—from which magazine Fitzgerald had received a number of advances for work not yet received. Gingrich, hoping to rouse Fitzgerald from his gloom and inactivity, explained that the auditors of *Esquire* were becoming troublesome about the novelist's account in the ledger books: money advanced, no work forthcoming. Could Fitzgerald produce something to relieve Gingrich's embarrassment? "Write anything," the editor advised: a manuscript of some kind—something to keep in the files—to placate the bookkeeping department. Fitzgerald reflected a moment and then agreed to Gingrich's proposal: "I'll write about why I can't write any more," he said. Soon afterward he sent Gingrich the manuscript of "The Crack-Up." And in the following months Fitzgerald turned out semistories— "Afternoon of an Author" and "Author's House"—which represent a bridge between the autobiography of "The Crack-Up" and the fiction he would again produce as he emerged from his slump.

Not long afterward he settled in Hollywood, where he commenced his "third act and epilogue"—a period of three and a half years that was not, as Mark Schorer claims in his recent biography of Sinclair Lewis, a time of "final isolation and despair," but rather a partially successful attempt to regain his old ability and self-confidence. There were still alcoholic outbursts, periods of debility and sickness, and other troubles; but he was producing again, and judging from his letters during this time he had recovered a large measure of his optimism and pride of craft. Budd Schulberg, who knew Fitzgerald during these years, confirms this impression: Fitzgerald was physically on the downgrade but creatively on the rise, Schulberg writes in a recent issue of *Esquire*. And he adds that Fitzgerald was as "ready" for the years to come—that is, emotionally and creatively eager to produce—as any writer Schulberg knew.

What happened to Fitzgerald in Hollywood seems clear enough. He had accepted a position with the studios because they offered him impressively high pay, which he could not hope to earn publishing fiction. His script-writing work left him little energy for more serious projects; but in 1939, by which time he had exhausted his supply of steady jobs at the studios, he turned again to fiction. "Never any luck with movies," he had written in 1936. "Stick to your last, boy." Fitzgerald had begun to emerge from his creative inertia; he was in earnest now; and he turned out a large number of short stories and made good progress on his Hollywood novel. Around this time he wrote to a friend that he was feeling a new "lust for life" again; "the gloom of all causes does not affect it—I feel a certain rebirth of kinetic impulses. . . ." Fitzgerald's "feeling of rebirth" signified his readiness for a new cycle of development.

But what did he produce during these last years? With only a few exceptions, Fitzgerald's short fiction in 1939-1940 is devoted to the Pat Hobby series (he wrote seventeen of these stories in all). Pat Hobby is a third- or fourth-string writer for the Hollywood studios—a character with a penchant for graceless behavior and bad luck. Fitzgerald's tone in these stories is half-ironic, half-tolerant, amused, and understanding. The details of studio life and the circumstances of Pat's down-and-not-quite-out existence are all there: the hero is a convincing creation, the setting is vividly and authoritatively presented. The Hobby stories are, in fact, extremely successful efforts—for what they are. But their effect is finally disappointing. Fitzgerald was not attempting anything significant in them, and significance is the one quality they surely lack. They are among the most trivial of Fitzgerald's works, and their triviality is the more conspicuous for their being the product of the novelist's mature years. Even the flimsiest of the early stories (see, for example, "Bernice Bobs Her Hair") conveys a more immediate sense of importance than these miniatures in the life of a Hollywood ne'er-do-well.

The Last Tycoon, of course, is another matter. Into his last novel Fitzgerald projected more than his perceptive awareness of life in Hollywood; even in its unfinished state the work suggests that Fitzgerald invested in its composition the fullest extent of his talent, intelligence, and experience. The hero's intense love affair, his struggle to maintain his empire against intrigue, unscrupulous competition, and a violently changing system of values and political attitudes—these aspects of content lend substance and seriousness to Fitzgerald's final effort. And although *The Last Tycoon* suggests no development on Fitzgerald's part, no new discoveries in the art of novel-making, the completed sections are informed by the spontaneous and inspired quality of his best fiction. It is obvious, then, that Fitzgerald was capable of distinguished work without the benefit of the stimulus provided in earlier years by Wilson, Mencken, Lardner, or Hemingway.

Yet there are strong indications that *The Last Tycoon* was the product of some such stimulation. If in the insignificant Pat Hobby stories Fitzgerald was drawing an exaggerated and cynical portrait of himself, in the more serious *Last Tycoon* he was portraying, at least in part, the Hollywood producer Irving Thalberg, a man for whom he felt profound respect. Fitzgerald's old habit of admiration apparently fixed itself on this young motion-picture genius, about whom he wrote in *The Last Tycoon*:

> He had flown up very high to see, on strong wings, when he was young. And while he was up there he had looked on all the kingdoms, with the kind of eyes that can stare straight into the sun. Beating his wings tenaciously—and keeping on beating them, he had stayed up there longer than most of us, and then, remembering all he had seen from his great height of how things were, he had settled gradually to earth.

To a large extent, of course, this is self-portraiture. In illustration we might compare the similar imagery Fitzgerald applied to himself in the story-essay "Author's House." The narrator of "Author's House" conducts his visitor to the turret, or watchtower of his residence and wistfully confesses: "I lived up here once. . . . For just a

little while when I was young." For further confirmation
we have Budd Schulberg's word that Monroe Stahr was
Thalberg "ingeniously combined with and romantically fil-
tered through the nature of Scott himself." We cannot say
what proportion of the admixture was Fitzgerald; but it is
clear that a large part of the characterization stemmed
from the novelist's fascination with the brilliant young
producer. In addition, it seems that Schulberg himself was
responsible for some of the material Fitzgerald incorporated into his last novel: Fitzgerald used several of the
younger writer's anecdotes about Hollywood life, and when
Schulberg later read the novel he found that Fitzgerald
had occasionally quoted him verbatim. Obviously the
imagination of the novelist was being stimulated in the
old way: he was fashioning his material after impressions
received from men whom he admired and with whom he
had enjoyed a personal-professional association.

At the same time, the fact that *The Last Tycoon* approxi-
mates the earlier style of *The Great Gatsby*,[2] suggests that
Fitzgerald failed to encounter a writer during this period
who might have inspired him to attempt a new manner or
mode of presenting his materials. Indeed, the Hollywood
writers Fitzgerald did encounter (with a few exceptions)
seemed to evoke a strong unfavorable reaction. To Gerald
Murphy, Fitzgerald wrote in 1940 that he had found no
interesting groups in Hollywood, that even after brief acquaintance one recognized that everywhere there was corruption or indifference, and that the heroes of the community were the great corruptionists or the supremely
indifferent—by whom he meant, Fitzgerald explained, the
spoiled writers of Hollywood. It is also evident that while

---

[2] A fact that Fitzgerald himself recognized in his "Notes" to *The
Last Tycoon:* "If one book could ever be 'like' another, I should say
it is more 'like' *The Great Gatsby* than any other of my books."

Schulberg and Thalberg provided some of the inspiration for *The Last Tycoon*, neither one represented the kind of influence that might have effected a reorientation of Fitzgerald's approach to his art.

Mention of Schulberg suggests another interesting aspect of Fitzgerald's life at this time, one that is closely related to the novelist's susceptibility to influence. If at the age of twenty or twenty-four or even thirty Fitzgerald had adopted the role of novice at the feet of the master, he must have found something incongruous about assuming the same position at the age of forty-two or -three. When he came to Hollywood he was not exactly an "established author"—he felt too poignantly the neglect and indifference of his public—but he was something of an old hand; and he had, among a small company of American readers, his devotees. It is difficult to escape the feeling that it was now the turn of the pupil to be the mentor, the time for the man who had been guided and influenced to become a guide and influence to others. It should be stated that Fitzgerald not only adopted this mature role willingly, but that he performed it with generosity and grace. There might have been some ambivalence to his performance, as when he accepted Schulberg's homage at the same time that he was picking his brain for Hollywood local color; but to novice writers like Charles Warren or the more accomplished Nathanael West, Fitzgerald offered assistance, when called upon, unreservedly.

It is possible, too, that he not only enjoyed the role of literary mentor, but that he felt, perhaps unconsciously, an urgent need to acquit himself well in it. Certainly Fitzgerald's relationship with Sheilah Graham—or one facet of it—may be interpreted in this light: he set her to a systematic reading of English and American classics, and he gave her instructions about keeping a notebook for future literary endeavors of her own.[3] At the same time his letters to his daughter (then a teen-age student at Vassar), with their repeated passages of advice on the art of reading and writing, display something of the same impulse. What he felt during those last years, apparently, was the onus of responsibility to serve and benefit others as he had been served and benefited all his life. His depiction of Monroe Stahr, finally, might be a reflection of this same temperamental need: Stahr is, above all, the man upon whom others depend professionally for guidance and judgment. We might profitably avail ourselves, once more, of Budd Schulberg's store of recollections: Fitzgerald was fascinated, Schulberg remembers, by Irving Thalberg's role as creative and intellectual prime minister of his mythical kingdom. Exactly so: the fascination was a part of the novelist's new self-image, and it found expression in the character of Stahr-Thalberg-Fitzgerald.

But perhaps, in conclusion, what really matters is that we see *The Last Tycoon* at some distance, as a literary and personal achievement wrought in defiance of time and difficulty. The years of loss had led to a recovery that was in its own way inspired; for within Fitzgerald were the still functioning powers upon which he had built an early and lasting glory. Upon that foundation he had fashioned a method typical of an epoch when American writers had forged vivid and memorable works of art; now he returned naturally to the method and spirit of that time. Had he lived he would have brought it off brilliantly in the end—as James Thurber remarked in his review of the unfinished *Last Tycoon*. But he would have "brought off" something more than a brilliant novel; there is always the suggestion, elusive but persistent, that Fitzgerald by his presence

[3] See Sheilah Graham, *Beloved Infidel* (New York, 1958), pp. 262-263, 284-285, 315.

would have illuminated a later period with the genius of a decade that for him was still a potent and living reality.

And what of the epilogue? Did he foresee that twenty years after his death students of American literature, both casual and serious, would render him homage and appreciation such as few of our writers have received? Perhaps he did; undoubtedly he hoped for it and aimed for it in his works. Fitzgerald accomplished more than a chronicle of Jazz Age belles and playboys, with whom he has been consistently associated. His repeated emphasis on the theme of corruptive wealth—present even in the notes for the unfinished parts of *The Last Tycoon*—and his depiction of the melancholy implications in the dream of the social aspirer—these represent the core of his commentary on our experience. His contribution was twofold: he distilled in beautiful prose the spirit of an age, and he urged a penetrating criticism of the values that formed its foundation. Fitzgerald saw clearly the optimism and materialism of democracy in America, forces which have characterized our history since its inception, and which continue to affect our attitudes and our conduct. These tendencies in our past and present find a focal point of argument in such works as *The Great Gatsby* and *Tender Is the Night*, rendered concretely and exquisitely by the fabulist of our mores, Scott Fitzgerald.

His debt to other writers was considerable, but another aspect of his endeavors must not be underestimated. Few writers as accomplished as Fitzgerald have performed in a vacuum—without the encouragement, stimulation, and inspiration of other authors. But none have achieved as much as he without solitary and independent effort. No doubt a great deal of what he wrote, and the way he wrote it, was the product of his association with men like Wilson, Mencken, Lardner, and Hemingway. But the essence of it was accomplished—as Fitzgerald's daughter has written—by "sweat," "heart-breaking effort," and "painful hours of work under the most adverse circumstances." No one "made" Scott Fitzgerald but himself.

Yet a record of his personal and professional relations with other writers illuminates his time, his life, and his art. That record might also serve as a representative example of literary sensibility and practice, at least in the sense that moved Henry James to observe:

> The best things come, as a general thing, from the talents that are members of a group; every man works better when he has companions working in the same line, and yielding the stimulus of suggestion, comparison, emulation. Great things of course have been done by solitary workers; but they have usually been done with double the pains they would have cost if they had been produced in more genial circumstances. The solitary worker loses the profit of example and discussion; he is apt to make awkward experiments; he is in the nature of the case more or less of an empiric. . . .

The best things come from the talents that are members of a group: assuredly, as the experience of Fitzgerald and his contemporaries proves. As an artist whose considerable talents flourished and prospered under the stimulus of "suggestion, comparison, emulation," Scott Fitzgerald will endure.

APPENDIX

The following letters, all of which are taken from the correspondence files of The F. Scott Fitzgerald Papers at Princeton Library, are examples of the tone of Fitzgerald's relations with literary people over the total span of his career. Several of them—such as those from James Branch Cabell, Thornton Wilder, and Louis Bromfield—are from writers to whom Fitzgerald was not particularly close; others reveal a deeper and more personal understanding between the correspondents. I have deliberately included here something of a random and varied sampling: the letters are from persons older and younger than Fitzgerald as well as from exact contemporaries, and they comment on works as different from each other as *This Side of Paradise, The Great Gatsby, Tender Is the Night,* and "The Crack-Up." But they all show the mutual interest and spirit that characterized Fitzgerald's life and his era.

Dec. 29, 1920

Dear Mr. Fitzgerald:

When I received your wife's delightful letter telling of her need of a copy of Jurgen against your Christmasing, I was doubly glad of my forethought in having laid in a small "private stock" between the time of the book's suppression and the time the news reached the Richmond dealers. It enabled me, you see, to express tangibly the interest and hopes awakened by This Side of Paradise— Oh, yes, I admired a great deal and quite cordially, but I optimistically insist upon regarding the book as a prophecy forerunning even finer books.

I hope—though probably that is asking too much of human nature at your time of life—that you will not be very much spoiled by the book's, quite merited, success. I can imagine no book which, in view of all the circumstances, could be more interesting reading than your second novel will be perforce. For you seem to have all the gifts. . . .

JAMES BRANCH CABELL

Dumbarton Grange
Dumbarton, Virginia

Jan. 12, 1928

I have been an admirer, not to say a student of The Great Gatsby too long not to have got a great kick out of your letter. It gives me the grounds to hope that we may sometime have some long talks on what writing's all about. As you see I am a provincial school-master and have always worked alone. And yet nothing interests me more than thinking of our generation as a league and as a protest to the whole cardboard generation that precedes us from Wharton through Cabell and Anderson and Sinclair Lewis.

THORNTON WILDER

Lawrenceville

Letter of Introduction to Tristan Tzara

25 May, 1928

M. et Mme. Scott Fitzgerald. Il est le romancier le plus doué non seulement de nos jeunes, mais de tous nos ecrivains, et quant à elle, vous verrez comme elle a une genie tout à fait particuliere.

GILBERT SELDES

Undated (c. 1934)

Dear Scott:

It is I should think permanent [the reference is to *Tender Is the Night*]. That we should see deeper into it than the older or younger reader is inevitable. They don't know what it's about. I've just embarked on a ponderous novel on the same theme. . . . I'm going the whole hog. My "hero," surrounded by all the blessings in the world, simply goes out to the garage and shoots himself—fifteen years after the war. Anyway it is all a fascinating business, this writing. As to the "younger generation" most of them seem pretty "arty" and self-conscious and the hard-boiled school is the most tiresome of all. Perhaps when they become middle-aged like ourselves they'll outgrow it. We did have [?] the Golden Age. Hot or cold, we were very lucky. I never knew it more profoundly than during the past winter when a lot of Princeton undergraduates crossed my path.

LOUIS BROMFIELD

Feb. 7, 1935

Dear Scott:

There was no one whose opinion on Act of Darkness I waited for with more eagerness and trepidation. You can guess, therefore, with what pleasure and appreciation I read your long and generous letter. . . .

The matter of influences I shall ponder. I have my weakness that way. The remark on p. 148 is Ernest's: I adopted it from his conversation, when I talked to him about leaving Hadley; I did not know he had used it in a book. Perhaps he hasn't, but it still shows that writers cannot prey on each other, even as living beings. And there are a number of Charlie's remarks which came from literary guys: three at least from Cummings. . . .

But I thank you from the bottom of my heart and from the top too and all the circumference for your kindness and your praise. It means so much to me that you approve the novel.   JOHN

John Peale Bishop

New Orleans, La.

June 2, 1935

I greatly appreciated your letter. You are one of the two or three people who are generous enough to be concerned with my literary career, and you have done more than anyone else to forward it. And of this I am constantly aware and for it most grateful. . . .   JOHN

John Peale Bishop

New Orleans, La.

Undated (c. 1936)

I've just finished "The Great Gatsby" again— You were wise so young— I'm only beginning to know some of the things you must have been born knowing— The book resolves itself into the strangest feeling of a crystal globe, or one of the immense soap bubbles we achieved as children, if it could hold its shape and color without breaking —it is so beautiful, it is so clairvoyant, it is so heartbreaking—   MARJORIE KINNAN RAWLINGS

Feb. 17, 1936

... being so completely in and of an era—for belonging so completely to the Jazz Age that when it went, I had to go. . . .

Never again do I expect to write anything that I shall not be slightly ashamed of.

That is the deepest hurt of these depths; to know that never again. . . .

The present age is such a *hollow* mess of futility. . . . We were futile, of course, but we had gusto, a certain peculiar tenderness, a funny kind of idealism, and a good deal of background. If we tried to kick standards in the ass, at least the standards were there. Now there's nothing except excruciating vulgarity and smart-aleckism.

JOHN V. A. WEAVER

Weaver, one of Fitzgerald's old friends from the twenties, wrote this letter soon after Fitzgerald's "Crack-Up" articles appeared in *Esquire*. Early paragraphs of the letter, omitted here, advise Fitzgerald that Weaver is in complete sympathy with Fitzgerald's pessimistic frame of mind during this period.

April 5, 1939

Dear Mr. Fitzgerald:

I never thanked you for your kindness to me in the preface to the Modern Library edition of "The Great Gatsby." When I read it, I got a great lift just at a time when I needed one badly, if I was to go on writing.

Somehow or other I seem to have slipped in between all the "schools." My books meet no needs except my own, their circulation is practically private and I'm lucky to be published. And yet, I only have a desire to remedy all that *before* sitting down to write, once begun I do it my way. I forget the broad sweep, the big canvas, the shot-gun adjectives, the important people, the significant ideas, the lessons to be taught, the epic Thomas Wolfe, the realistic James Farrell;—and go on making what one critic called "private and unfunny jokes." Your preface made me feel that they weren't completely private and maybe not even entirely jokes. NATHANAEL WEST

West died on December 22, 1940—one day after the death of Fitzgerald. The previous year Fitzgerald had praised West's works in his Introduction to the Modern Library edition of *The Great Gatsby*.

BIBLIOGRAPHY

In addition to primary sources cited in the text—the works of Fitzgerald, Wilson, Mencken, Lardner, and Hemingway —I have used numerous secondary sources in the preparation of this study. Below I list the books and articles which provide pertinent commentary, and upon which I drew for each chapter. I should begin by acknowledging my debt to Arthur Mizener's biography *The Far Side of Paradise,* Cambridge, Mass.: Houghton Mifflin Company, 1951, which I used consistently, from beginning to end. Occasionally I also drew upon Andrew Turnbull's recent work *Scott Fitzgerald,* New York: Scribner's, 1962; but the major portion of my book was completed before Mr. Turnbull's biography was released.

CHAPTER I

Allen, Frederick Lewis. *Only Yesterday.* New York: Harper & Brothers, 1931.

Boyd, Ernest. *Portraits: Real and Imaginary.* New York: George H. Doran, 1924.

Civilization in the United States: An Inquiry by Thirty

Americans. Edited by Harold Stearns. New York: Harcourt, Brace & Company, 1922.

Cleaton, Irene and Allen. *Books and Battles*. Boston: Houghton Mifflin Company, 1937.

Cowley, Malcolm. *Exile's Return*. New York: The Viking Press, Inc., 1956.

——. "The Generation That Wasn't Lost," *College English*, V:5 (February, 1944), 233-239.

Hoffman, Frederick J. *The Twenties: American Writing in the Post-war Decade*. New York: The Viking Press, Inc., 1955.

Horton, Philip. *Hart Crane: The Life of an American Poet*. New York: The Viking Press, Inc., 1957.

Kazin, Alfred. *On Native Grounds: An Interpretation of Modern American Prose Literature*. New York: Doubleday & Co., Inc., 1956 (originally published in 1942).

Kroeber, A. L. *Configurations of Culture Growth*. Berkeley, Calif.: University of California Press, 1944.

Lippmann, Walter. *A Preface to Morals*. New York: The Macmillan Co., 1929.

The Literary Spotlight. Edited by John Farrar. New York: George H. Doran, 1924.

Loeb, Harold. *The Way It Was*. New York: Criterion Books, Inc., 1959.

Lynd, Robert S. and Helen Merrill. *Middletown: A Study in American Culture*. New York: Harcourt, Brace & Co., 1929.

Stein, Gertrude. *The Autobiography of Alice B. Toklas*. New York: Harcourt, Brace & Co., 1933.

Stewart, Donald Ogden. *A Parody Outline of History*. New York: George H. Doran, 1921.

Tocqueville, Alexis de. *Democracy in America*. Edited by Phillips Bradley. 2 vols. New York: Vintage Books, Inc., 1954.

CHAPTER II

Aldridge, John W. *After the Lost Generation*. New York: The Noonday Press, 1958.

F. Scott Fitzgerald: The Man and His Work. Edited by Alfred Kazin. New York: The World Publishing Co., 1951.

Gauss, Christian. "Edmund Wilson: The Campus and the Nassau 'Lit,'" *Princeton University Library Chronicle*, V:2 (February, 1944), 41-50.

——. *The Papers of Christian Gauss*. Edited by Katherine Gauss Jackson and Hiram Haydn. New York: Random House, 1957.

Piper, Henry Dan. "F. Scott Fitzgerald: A Check List," *Princeton University Library Chronicle*, XII:4 (Summer, 1951), 201-202.

——. "Scott Fitzgerald and the Origins of the Jazz Age." Unpublished Ph.D. dissertation, University of Pennsylvania, 1950.

Wilson, Edmund. *Classics and Commercials*. New York: Farrar, Straus and Young, Inc., 1951.

——. *The Shores of Light*. New York: Farrar, Straus and Young, Inc., 1952.

CHAPTER III

Angoff, Charles. *H. L. Mencken: A Portrait from Memory*. New York: T. Yoseloff, 1956.

Goldberg, Isaac. *The Man Mencken*. 2 vols. New York: Simon and Schuster, Inc., 1925.

Hoffman, Frederick J. *The Little Magazine: A History and a Bibliography*. Princeton: Princeton University Press, 1946.

Kemler, Edgar. *The Irreverent Mr. Mencken*. Boston, Mass.: Atlantic-Little, Brown, 1950.

Manchester, William. *Disturber of the Peace: The Life of H. L. Mencken.* New York: Harper & Brothers, 1951.

Miller, James E., Jr. *The Fictional Technique of Scott Fitzgerald.* The Hague: M. Nijhoff, 1957.

CHAPTER IV

Elder, Donald. *Ring Lardner.* New York: Doubleday and Co., Inc., 1956.

Geismar, Maxwell. *Writers in Crisis.* Boston: Houghton Mifflin Co., 1942.

Piper, Henry Dan. "Scott Fitzgerald and the Origins of the Jazz Age." Unpublished Ph.D. dissertation, University of Pennsylvania, 1950.

Soule, George. *Prosperity Decade: From War to Depression: 1917-1929.* (The Economic History of the United States, Vol. III.) New York: Rinehart & Co., Inc., 1947.

Yates, Donald A. "Fitzgerald and Football," *Michigan Alumnus Quarterly Review,* LXIV: 10 (Autumn, 1957), 75-80.

CHAPTER V

Baker, Carlos. *Hemingway: The Writer As Artist.* Princeton: Princeton University Press, 1956.

——. "Hemingway," *Saturday Review,* XLIV:30 (July 29, 1961), 11-12.

Brooks, Van Wyck. *The Writer in America.* New York: E. P. Dutton & Co., 1953.

Burlingame, Roger. *Of Making Many Books.* New York: Charles Scribner's Sons, 1946.

Cargill, Oscar. *Intellectual America: Ideas on the March.* New York: The Macmillan Co., 1941.

Eliot, T. S. *The Complete Poems and Plays.* New York: Harcourt, Brace & Co., 1952.

Fenton, Charles A. *The Apprenticeship of Ernest Heming-way*. New York: The Viking Press, Inc., 1958.

Fiedler, Leslie A. *Love and Death in the American Novel*. New York: Criterion Books, 1960.

Graham, Sheilah and Gerold Frank. *Beloved Infidel: The Education of a Woman*. New York: Henry Holt and Co., Inc., 1958.

Ernest Hemingway: The Man and His Work. Edited by John K. M. McCaffery. New York: The World Publishing Co., 1956.

Hindus, Milton. "F. Scott Fitzgerald and Literary Anti-Semitism," *Commentary*, III (June, 1947), 508-516.

Josephson, Matthew. *Portrait of the Artist as American*. New York: Harcourt, Brace & Co., 1930.

Kuehl, John Richard. "Scott Fitzgerald: Romantic and Realist." Unpublished Ph.D. dissertation, Columbia University, 1958.

——. "Scott Fitzgerald's Reading," *Princeton University Library Chronicle*, XXII:2 (Winter, 1961), 58-89.

Lawrence, D. H. *Studies in Classic American Literature*. New York: Doubleday and Co., Inc., 1951 (originally published in the United States in 1923).

Nathan, George Jean. "The Golden Boy of the Twenties," *Esquire*, L:4 (October, 1958), 148-149.

Piper, Henry Dan. "Scott Fitzgerald and the Origins of the Jazz Age." Unpublished Ph.D. dissertation, University of Pennsylvania, 1950.

Rideout, Walter B. *The Radical Novel in the United States: 1900-1954*. Cambridge, Mass.: Harvard University Press, 1956.

Tynan, Kenneth. "A Visit to Havana," *Holiday*, 27:2 (February, 1960), 50-58.

Young, Philip. *Ernest Hemingway*. New York: Rinehart & Company, Inc., 1952.

CHAPTER VI

Graham, Sheilah and Gerold Frank. *Beloved Infidel: The Education of a Woman.* New York: Henry Holt and Co., Inc., 1958.

James, Henry. "Hawthorne," *The Shock of Recognition.* Edited by Edmund Wilson. New York: Doubleday and Co., 1943.

Schulberg, Budd. *The Disenchanted.* New York: Random House, 1950.

———. "Old Scott: The Mask, the Myth, and the Man," *Esquire,* LV:1 (January, 1961), 96-101.

INDEX

243

ABOUT THE AUTHOR

William Goldhurst was born in New York City on August 8, 1929. He has degrees from Kenyon College and Columbia University, and from Tulane University, where he took his Ph.D. in 1962. Mr. Goldhurst has taught at Ohio State University, Tulane, and Newcomb College, and is now Assistant Professor of English at the University of Puerto Rico. He lives in Rio Piedras, Puerto Rico, with his wife and two sons.

THIS BOOK WAS SET IN
CALEDONIA AND DELPHIN TYPES BY
THE HARRY SWEETMAN TYPESETTING CORPORATION.
IT WAS PRINTED AND BOUND AT THE PRESS OF
THE WORLD PUBLISHING COMPANY.
DESIGN IS BY JACK JAGET.